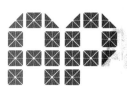

Models:

Published in Great Britain in 2006 by Wiley-Academy
a division of John Wiley & Sons Ltd

Copyright © 2006 John Wiley & Sons Ltd, The Atrium,
Southern Gate, Chichester, West Sussex PO19 8SQ, UK
Telephone +44 (0)1243 779 777

Email (for orders & customer service enquiries): cs-books@wiley.co.uk
Visit our Home Page on www.wiley.co.uk or www.wiley.com

This publication is designed to provide accurate and authorative
information in regard to the subject matter covered. It is sold on
the understanding that the Publisher is not engaged in rendering
professional services. If professional advice or other expert
assistance is required, the services of a competent professional
should be sought.

Other Wiley Editorial Offices

John Wiley & Sons Inc., 111 River Street, Hoboken,
NJ 07030, USA

Jossey-Bass, 989 Market Street, San Francisco,
CA 94103-1741, USA

Wiley-VCH Verlag GmbH, Boschstraße 12,
D-69469 Weinheim, Germany

John Wiley & SOns Australia Ltd, 42 McDougall Street,
Milton, Queensland 4064, Australia

John Wiley & Sons (Asia) Pte Ltd, 2 Clement Loop,
#02-01, Jin Xing Distripark, Singapore 129809

John Wiley & Sons Canada Lyd, 5353 Dundas Street West,
Suite 400, Etobicoke, Ontario M9B 6H8, Canada

ISBN-13 978 0 470 01592 6
ISBN-10 0 470 01592 6

Cover Design by Ian Lambot Studio, UK

Designed by Ian Lambot Studio, UK
Printed and bound by Grafos SA, Spain

Architecture in Practice

Models: Architecture and the Miniature

Mark Morris

WILEY-ACADEMY

Contents

Introduction
To 3D or Not to 3D

Why should architects use models?

If, by model, we mean those small-scale objects usually cluttering an architect's studio, this question seems reasonable given the profession's adoption of computer-aided design. Three decades ago the same question was asked in a pre-digital environment by a group of young up-and-comers mounting an exhibition in Manhattan. In 1976, under the auspices of the Institute for Architecture and Urban Studies, Peter Eisenman and Charles Gwathmey mounted the 'Idea as Model' show, which marked the first time models were exhibited and studied exclusively as more than mere props:

> It seemed that models, like architectural drawings, could well have an artistic or conceptual existence of their own, one which was relatively independent of the project that they represented. In 1976, as a result of this initial interest, the Institute decided to mount an exhibition whose prime intent was to test and then demonstrate this hypothesis of the conceptual model.[1]

This extended the argument put forward in the original letter sent to request models for the exhibit. *"The purpose of this exhibition is to clarify new means of investigating architecture in three-dimensional form. We do not seek to assemble models of buildings as propaganda for persuading clients, but rather as studies of a hypothesis, a problem, or an idea of architecture."*[2] The Institute included Charles Gwathmey as president, Frank Gehry and Philip Johnson among others as trustees, and Diana Agrest, Julia Bloomfield, Kenneth Frampton and Tony Vidler as fellows. The catalogue featured work by Robert Venturi, Robert Stern, Michael Graves, Leon Krier, Aldo Rossi, Hans Hollein, John Hejduk, Richard Meier, Rafael Moneo, Charles Moore, Jaquelin Robertson, Robert Stern, Stanley Tigerman and Simon Ungers, along with projects by the trustees, fellows and president. Most of the (future) leading lights of architecture were folded into the Idea as Model project.[3]

The definitive catalogue for 'Idea as Model' came four years after the fact and reframed the exhibition from the vantage point of the very start of the 1980s, a decade which would see the advent of computer modelling. Published in 1981, however, *Idea as Model* was a pre-digital analysis, its considerations untroubled by the coming changes in media. The Institute was concerned with *"… the idea of the model as a conceptual as opposed to narrative tool, as part of the design process"*.[4] Models need not merely describe a project, but generate it.

Yet years later Diana Agrest wrote: *"Architecture is produced in three different registers, through three different texts; drawing, writing, and building."*[5] She footnotes this assertion with, *"we could count four, if we consider models"*. But architects and academics tend not to consider models; we relegate them to footnotes. We use models – as design tools, in education, to win commissions – but we do not consider them. Models may dominate academic activity, competitions and aspects of practice, but they do not dominate the discourse, they footnote it. Here the effort is to extend that footnote specifically targeting the model's relationship to size, scale and the effects of the miniature.

Opposite
Exhibit at the Excited Volumes /
Liverpool Biennale Symposium,
Static Gallery, 2002. The
camera offers an easy object
lesson in scale and relative
measurement

Terms and Conditions

'Model' is a surprisingly flexible term even for architects, so much so that it is rarely seen in dictionaries of architecure.[6] Model applies to a whole gamut of real and virtual objects, running from what appear to be crumpled up wads of paper to models so highly finished that they appear as real full-scale buildings in photographs, and to a growing array of digital types that, by layers or in sequence, target a myriad of design concerns. For clarity, one could note the difference between old school or analogue models – that is, touchable scale models versus virtual models – but the development of digitally fabricated models cut by laser, router or built up by a three-dimensional printer blurs this distinction. Even if one accepts the labels for analogue and digital models, each of these is an umbrella term for several more model types. One could elect to categorise in terms of performativity or functionality: what a given model is built to specifically do. This would blur analogue and digital more. But there are differences between the analogue and digital and between type, some more obvious, others more intangible. Categorising what these differences are and what they could mean to the creative process provides a path to employing any model more effectively.

Assumptions regarding any model are fairly straightforward: for example, (1) models represent buildings; (2) models are at a smaller scale than the buildings that they represent; and (3) models make it easy to comprehend the architectural idea. While not entirely rejecting these, counter cases might be put forward arguing that (1) models are not always representational; (2) size must be considered in relation to scale; and (3) rather than being a technique for translating design into built form, the model directly enters the design process.

The model is a good workhorse, a tool. A decade ago, it seemed the traditional scale model was on its way out, replaced by other kinds of architectural representation like cinematic digital fly-throughs and highly rendered perspectives of virtual models – useful new tools to be sure. But thanks to three-dimensional rendering technologies, the tactile model is enjoying a comeback. Certainly, computer-aided manufacture or CAM models might recapture attributes of scale models in terms of our reception of them. In large part, CAM models look like highly finished old school scale models. On the other hand, CAM models eschew the rather primitive techniques employed in the making of tradtional scale models. Those techniques – tracing, cutting, folding, pasting – held certain possibilities their digital replacements alter or forgo. Moreover, while CAM models may be small-scaled, they are prepared in a digital environment that nominally operates at full-scale. In other words, while both analogue and CAM models might in fact be small, the analogue is conceived from the start at a scale, as something small.

Thinking Small

Christian Hubert's opening remarks in his essay for *Idea as Model* caution *"size and scale are not to be confused,"* [7] but they often are. Technically, size is quantitative and bound to measurement while scale is qualitative and relative – something is bigger than something else. Yet the everyday misuse of these terms, that confusion, offers other insights. Measurement sets up scalar relationships. Proportion, for example, would seem an instance of size and scale overlapping, where measurable interrelations are independent of size and can be of any scale. Scale, by contrast, entails the existence of other entities or elements to which the object is compared. Thus, we can say that a model is in a different scale than the real building – but we can also talk about 'scale models' or say that a map or a diagram of a building is 'not drawn to scale', meaning that the different parts of the same object (model or drawing) do not relate to each other one to one. So long as a model is consistently to a scale, it seems beside the point that it should be referred to as small in relation to what it means to represent.

But why are architectural models usually small-scale? [8] Assumptions regarding certain economies seem straightforward. **Cost**. A very basic economy, not only is the model cheaper to build than a real building, it saves the cost of pulling down or altering a poorly planned real building. **Time**. Small models are quick to build, their diminution can be taken as abbreviation in a sense. The model saves time again with the building process overall, helping estimate real material issues and stages of construction. **Effort.** This can be taken several ways. While a real building is a collaborative work between architect, engineer, construction crew and so on, a model can be a remote and individual undertaking concentrating effort in one architect or small group of designers. Models also help check deficiencies in design and in their refinement curb the effort of imagining various problems only in drawing.

But there is another assumption tied to the model that is not really about economy. This has to do with ideas regarding process or stages of development that assume preliminary things are supposed to be smaller, simpler and less real than 'finished' things. One thinks of a painter's initial sketch refined and enlarged in various studies, cartoons and, finally, rendered on canvas. Or, as a biological metaphor, a baby growing, learning and becoming fully an adult. There is an intuitive sense that the small is preliminary or unfinished. In accordance with a whole logic of classification, two disparate qualities – size and preliminariness – are yoked together in the case of architectural representation, particularly in the case of models.

Rudolf Arnheim offers the term, 'thought model'. Not a sketch model, not even a material object, Arnheim imagines architects think in model-form, to scale:

No doubt, the architect must imagine with some degree of precision what the actual building will look like when approached from the street or seen from the inside. But much of the actual shaping must be done on thought models of the whole building, mental images that are supported sooner or later by small-scale models built at the office. [...] What can be seen in imagination tends, of course, to be less detailed and more generalized, but nevertheless the handling of a mental image bears a striking resemblance to the manipulation of an actual model with one's hands.[9]

But as soon as the scalar is framed in terms of architectural thought, Arnheim points out the ramifications of such in allometric terms: *"The advantages of using models are evident. To avoid being misled, however, the architect must keep in mind that the final product of his labours is a huge structure to be seen and used by small creatures. The difference between a small model and an actual building may lead to psychological discrepancies ..."*[10] That is to say, discrepancies between scalar thought and real-sized buildings, the gap between being filled by the scale model itself.

For Claude Lévi-Strauss any economies offered by the miniature are first and foremost the result of aesthetic aims. What, then, are the benefits of miniaturisation outside economic considerations?

Being smaller, the object as a whole seems less formidable. By being quantitatively diminished, it seems to us qualitatively simplified. More exactly, the quantitative transposition extends and diversifies our power over a homologue of the thing, and by means of it the latter can be grasped, assessed and apprehended at a glance.[11]

Lastly, Lévi-Strauss connects ease of apprehension with some notion of power over something 'formidable'. Through the miniature, a sort of conceptual victory can be had:

In the case of miniatures, in contrast to what happens when we try to understand an object or living creature of real dimensions, knowledge of the whole precedes knowledge of the parts. And even if this is an illusion, the point of the procedure is to create or sustain the illusion, which gratifies the intelligence and gives rise to a sense of pleasure which can already be called aesthetic on these grounds alone." [12]

It is a fundamentally different way of coming to know something. Rather than work up to something unwieldy through easy-to-digest bits, the scaled down offers instant totality and a subsequent unravelling of detail. It would seem by taking the effort to make a model, its reception as an object requires almost no effort at all. This is spring-loaded comprehension, the intellectual 'buzz' of which cashes out as an immediate aesthetic experience.

Gaston Bachelard, within the context of literary criticism, offers that the small conjures up infinity more easily than the large. Indeed, the small, in certain instances, is the only way to create the sublime or to express large ideas. Only through the small can we really think about the truly large:

Such formulas as: being-in-the-world and world-being are too majestic for me and I do not succeed in experiencing them. In fact, I feel more at home in miniature worlds, which, for me, are dominated worlds. And when I live them I feel waves of world-consciousness emanating from my dreaming self. For me, the vastness of the world had become merely the jamming of these waves." [13]

A sense of delight is elaborated by Bachelard's exultation of the sublime of the small: *"Miniature is an exercise that has metaphysical freshness; it allows us to be world conscious at slight risk. And how restful this exercise on a dominated world can be! For miniature rests us without ever putting us to sleep. Here the imagination is both vigilant and content".* [14] Miniature runs together a density of information, proof of craft and an invitation to the subject to know something without yet really knowing it:

The cleverer I am at miniaturising the world, the better I possess it. But in doing this, it must be understood that the values become condensed and enriched in miniature. Platonic dialectics of large and small do not suffice for us to become cognizant of the dynamic virtues of miniature thinking. One must go beyond logic in order to experience what is large in what is small." [15]

Architects must take this illogical view when fashioning models, otherwise the practice would appear foolish; and clients, not to mention students of architecture, must be coaxed into this way of 'miniature thinking' without naming it as such.

As an object the model itself has a context, a site, a relationship to the environment it happens to be placed in. The impetus for the Idea as Model exhibition would seem to be rooted in simply moving objects normally housed in architects' offices to the space of a gallery. Some models can be handheld, possessed sensually, turned round in front of the eye according to the whims of its beholder. As an object in the world, it can be archived with other objects, gather dust, be lost, found, restored and researched. In this it claims a certain insularity, could be said to be semi-autonomous; never completely apart from the benefits and disadvantages of just *stuff*; it need never completely weigh anchor from the world of objects.

Models as objects are a bit ordinary, rooted enough in the everyday to seem familiar, formally intense enough to seem sublime in the context of everything else.

The pairing of the architectural and the miniature offers certain residuals that exceed those attributable to size or scale alone. One of these is representational and involves the visual density of information. Eugene Kupper puts it this way: *"Buildings seldom have the clarity-in-complexity that a model shows. Models gain energy by being small"*.[16] Others caution that this same quality can be a hindrance:

> *"By working directly in space, albeit at small scale, concepts are formed and reshaped as a result of their exploration in three-dimensions; a process in which options remain open in design routes – options which might not appear available to the designer trapped within the confines of paper. However, one significant drawback of scale models is their rich displays of spatial intricacy which can sidetrack the designer into a fascination with 'miniaturism' – an attitude associated with the discrepancy between human and model scales. This effect puts the designer outside the concept by interposing a distance known as the 'Gulliver Gap'."*[17]

One could argue that if there is such a thing as a Gulliver Gap, it is that gap wherein most architecture is conceived. It is only through such an interposed distance and with a sensibility facilitated by miniaturism that many projects are created. Rather than putting *"the designer outside the concept"*, it seems it is one of the chief ways into architectural concepts.

Opposite
Academic crit, The University
of North Carolina at Charlotte,
2004. Dreaded but effective,
the quasi-public critique
(bound to ritual, rhetoric and
pre-professional salesmanship)
is a relatively new teaching
method in architecture. Beaux-
Arts critiques were for critics
only, while the Bauhaus
preferred even more open
debate. No matter the project,
no matter the scope of the
presentation, if a model is
offered it tends to become the
focus of the discussion and
the primary sign of the work
whether intended or not

Some Disadvantages:

- Traditional models take time, money, special materials and certain levels of craft
- Unlike the virtual sort, they are sometimes awkward to revise
- As opposed to drawings or digital files, scale models are notoriously difficult to archive, they rarely keep well
- Quick apprehension of a scale model can lead some to misinterpret or come to wrong conclusions about the intent of a project
- Models readily reveal any gaps in a project's development and open up more apects of a project to criticism.

Some Advantages:

- Models communicate well. They hold a particular fascination for the non-architect as they are often the first manifestation of a design that a lay person can readily apprehend
- Models can sell a project in part by playing to the vanity of a client. By virture of their small scale, the model simultaneously empowers the viewer, what we might call the 'King Kong Effect'
- A model triggers memories or associations of childhood: models resemble toys, recall Lilliputian fantasies
- The whole is apprehended in advance of the parts, the 'big idea' can predominate any judgment of the project
- Being realised in three-dimensions, no matter how small, the model suggests the project is already a little bit real, or more real than the project presented in plans, sections and so on.

Opposite
Saint Stephan of Hungary
approving a model cathedral

A Model Education

Any early history of the model is spotty for the same reason model definitions are hard to come by, there is confusion about what counts as a model. Things like models have been found in ancient Egyptian tombs, model visions of the afterlife. Clay funerary pots shaped like temples have been plucked from dig sites throughout Greece. Burial jewellery resembling porticoes and stepped pyramids can be traced to extinct cultures in the Americas. Roman triumphs included models of captured cities paraded on horse-drawn carts before the emperor. There is evidence for occasional use of models during the Middle Ages. Yet historians quibble about whether these objects were indeed models in the architectural sense rather than symbolic objects. Depictions of saints and angels holding models of churches are common, but these are often signs of a donation to the church. Templates, precedent and full-scale mock-ups were useful training tools for medieval masons. The model, as architects understand it, was primarily a Renaissance invention.

To be sure, the drawing and not the model was the focus of Renaissance architectural treatises. Drawings were identified as the special domain of the architect, the principal means of communicating architectural intentions. As drawings were codified as abstract representations, models could be fashioned to more easily convey a design to patrons and the craftspeople charged with actual building. Models, therefore, usually played a supporting role to drawings conceptually.

Leon Battista Alberti was the earliest, clearest and most forceful advocate of the model as a design tool. The scale model is mentioned in classical texts[1] and treated later by Vasari and Brunelleschi, but Alberti elaborates and crystallises the notion of the model not just as a medium of architectural expression, but as the primary vehicle of the design process. He starts by insisting that the model has precedent in Antiquity, which there is evidence for, and points firstly to its practical and social aspects:

Left
Engraving of Leon Battista
Alberti (1404 -1472). The re-
inventor of perspective also
re-invented the idea of the
architectural model still potent
today. Perspective and scale
models are both tied to
representation and diminution

I therefore always highly commend the ancient custom of builders, who not only in draughts and paintings, but in real models of wood or other substance, examined and weighed over and over again, with the advice of men of the best experience, the whole work and the ad-measurements of its parts, before they put themselves to the expense or trouble. By making a model you will have the opportunity, thoroughly to weigh and consider the form and situation ... .[2]

He then elaborates on the model's ability to suggest and take amendments and suggests its path to ideality: *"And there you may easily and freely add, retrench, alter, renew, and in short change every thing from one end to the other, till all and every one of the parts are just as you would have them, and without fault."* [3]

Just as Alberti insists on the model's possible strengths, he cautions against its fetishisation as an object and suggests the architect's self image is already bound up in the model. He recognizes, too, that the model may not be directly crafted by the architect and compares the architect and the painter on the basis of illusion, implying that the model is, despite its scale, more real than a drawing:

I must not omit to observe, that the making of curious, polished models, with the delicacy of the painting, is not required from an architect that only designs to show the real thing itself; but is rather the part of a vain architect, that makes it his business by charming the eye and striking the fancy of the beholder, to divert him from a rigorous examination of the parts which he ought to make, and to draw him into an admiration of himself.[4]

Lastly, Alberti puts in a caveat about time and novelty. He argues that even a 'perfected' model can be put aside and reviewed later as a means to test a good design:

To conclude, when the whole model and the contrivance of all the parts greatly pleases both yourself and others of good experience, so that you have not the least doubt remaining within yourself, and do not know of any thing that wants the least re-examination; even then I would advise you not to run furiously to the execution out of a passion for building … but if you will hearken to me, lay the thoughts of it aside for some time, till this favourite invention grows old. Then take a fresh review of everything, when not being guided by the fondness of your invention, but by the truth and reason of things you will be capable of judging more clearly.[5]

Alberti suggests that models be judged by other experts as well as being constantly examined by the designer. Not only does the model have practical benefits (in estimating materials, costs and division of labour in actual building), but for Alberti the model is a new and effective tool to arrive at a design, draw debate and through a lengthy process over time arrive at better and better schemes. Almost as an afterthought he realises a danger in the scale model and warns *"not to undertake a thing, which is above the power of man to do …"*. With the model he speaks to an array of still-current issues: social and professional aspects, as a sign of vanity or charlatanism, a means towards perfection through review and change, and simultaneously a trap and a check for novelty. Alberti in 1452 augments any previous conception of the model and sets parameters for subsequent model critique. Making the model a conceptual device for the architect rather than just a prop for the client was a defining shift in model thinking and one that still persists as a new idea.

Beaux-Arts to Bauhaus

The Albertian model and its notion of a three-dimensional design process was not fully realised until the early twentieth century. Surviving late-Renaissance and Baroque models often drift toward the polished and rhetorical, as with various schemes for St Peter's. Drawings, particularly the perspective, eclipsed models as the favoured form of architectural representation. This was in large part due to the erosion of the model's standing both in education and practice throughout the long span of the Academy in Paris. Colin Rowe claimed only two educational systems for architecture ever *"enjoyed a conspicuous success – those of the École des Beaux-Arts and the Bauhaus …"*.[6]

Rowe also noted they were treated as being mutually exclusive: *"According to present critical patterns the first influence is now condemned and the second is identified with the Enlightenment and progress. In the general understanding the first is associated with a derivative classicism and the second with the authentic tradition of modern architecture. Such an interpretation should not impede an analysis of their respective merits."*[7] Any look at a school of architecture today would suggest that both systems persist side by side, however uneasily. Architecture schools, largely made up of elements drawn from the École des Beaux-Arts and the Bauhaus, meld together two opposing pedagogical systems. Architecture school, as we know it, is a creation of the nineteenth century, but models as part of an official curriculum emerge only in the twentieth. Modern architectural education is an Anglo-American invention drawn from aristocratic French and revolutionary German sources.

The French Academy dominated architectural training for some two hundred years. Set up in opposition to guilds, a medieval system not under direct royal control, the idea was to elevate certain professions – architects, sculptors, painters – from craftsmen to philosophers based on idealised Renaissance academies. As the professional architect came to be defined

Left
Collection of designs at the
École des Beaux-Arts, 1882.
No models allowed

by the academy, there was pressure to separate the architect from the craftsman, carpenter or mason. The professional did not get his hands dirty, increasingly did not study construction and eventually divorced himself even from model making. The architecture studio resembled the painting studio, a world of two-dimensional representation.

The École des Beaux-Arts was based on the principle that there was a true architecture and that architecture was Greco-Roman: columns, cornices, pediments. This kit of parts was sacrosanct and the study of architecture was defined as the art of deploying these parts for various purposes. One problem, however, was that new building types were emerging at the end of the nineteenth-century – railway stations, for instance – and Neoclassicism was hard pressed to formulate convincing answers to new design questions.

As a way of creating an exercise in paper patterns this [Beaux-Arts] procedure is not unreasonable and, indeed, where the end in view is an exercise in the Sublime, it is quite appropriate. But as the mode of origin of a piece of architecture – a work of Practical Art – it is deeply perverse. And yet it became an unchallenged practice in schools of architecture throughout the world. [8]

The only time the word 'model' appears in Beaux-Arts curricula is when it refers to a cast architectural detail taken from a classical ruin and used as a drawing subject for entering students. On a practical level, the standard Beaux-Arts presentation drawing – a plan, section and perspective – allowed for easy transport, display and storage.

The export of Beaux-Arts architectural training was remarkably successful. As a method of instruction and state-sanctioned professionalisation, the Beaux-Arts system was adopted throughout Europe, its colonial possessions and in the europhile United States. Once in place, progress was along the lines of refinement rather than experimentation. There was some threat to the École des Beaux-Arts from the French Revolution and then Napoleon, but it existed more or less intact until the riots of 1968.

With the establishment of many Beaux-Arts inspired architecture programs in the nineteenth century, models were not excluded from school, but they were never required or prized in their own right. They might have been useful in solving certain compositional massing problems, but given the stranglehold of Neoclassicism, there was little room for spatial or decorative inventiveness and, therefore, no great need of models. Some even felt models to be a form of cheating. The art of plan drawing was so valued in Beaux-Arts training, that to create outside of that was taboo. For generations American applicants to the Paris or Rome Prize had to submit their standardised drawings in set dimensions in India ink. It would take a complete break from classicism to require models in official curricula.

The lack of interest shown in the model by the École des Beaux-Arts grew out of the Renaissance identification of the architect with drawing. This pairing stressed the notion of design as a pure idea, one which could be committed to paper as a form of notation not unlike text or a piece of music. Modelling was associated with sculpture, the *maquette*, which claimed its own territory elsewhere in the academy. The drawing's curious combination of specificity and ambiguity, its professional elitism and economy trumped the model as it remained an elaboration of a set of drawings. In this Beaux-Arts stance, the model was largely redundant. While a drawing could focus on form to the exclusion of materiality, a model seemed to wallow in matter even when it adhered to Alberti's model rules which emphasised form to the exclusion of anything else.

Turning Point: the Bauhaus

The École des Beaux-Arts in Paris enjoyed its largest numbers of American applicants in the years after the First World War and could be said to be at its height in terms of worldwide influence. At the same time, another school was taking shape in the newly founded Weimar Republic. Walter Gropius was persuaded to take over the Weimar School of Arts and Crafts from Henri van de Velde in 1919. Reorganising the Arts and Crafts school along with the Academy of Fine Art, Gropius founded the Bauhaus, literally House of Building, *"… bridging the disastrous gulf between reality and idealism."* [9] From the outset Gropius promised *"a*

Opposite
Model of the Bauhaus by the
College of Architecture, The
University of North Carolina
at Charlotte, 2003. A model
architecture school? The
Bauhaus at Dessau, Germany,
is a popular precedent for
students to model, but is this
because the Bauhaus curriculum promoted modelling or
because Gropius' design is just
easier to model than others?

Left
The model of Tatlin's Tower, of
1919, sufficed as a revolutionary architectural statement.
The model itself was famous,
featured at a party conference
and in parades. Vladimir Tatlin
claimed to work at 'laboratory
scale', a sensibility shared at/
borrowed from the Bauhaus

unification of the arts under the primacy of architecture". Oddly, architecture as such did not become a specific curriculum strand until eight years later. The model, however, was there from the start as part of the Bauhaus manifesto and revolutionary foundation course, the *Vorkurs*, as crafted by Gropius and school guru Johannes Itten.

> *The tool of the spirit of yesterday was the 'academy.' Academic training, however, brought about the development of a great proletariat destined to social misery. But the academy was too firmly established: practical training never advanced beyond dilettantism, and draughted and rendered 'design' remained in the foreground. … The hand masters matter through the crafts, and with the help of tools and machinery. Conception and visualisation are always simultaneous. Intellectual education runs parallel to manual training. Instruction in the theory of form is carried on in close contact with manual training.* [10]

Gropius and Itten could not have been more different. Gropius, progressive but respectable, was well-connected and had his own successful practice. Itten, with his shaved head, wearing a uniform of long purple robes, was a vegetarian, took regular enemas and punctured his skin to eliminate impurities as part of his adherence to various cults. Together they created a unique curriculum for the *Vorkurs* (or fore-course) meant to ground all in-coming students of arts, crafts or architecture in the fundamentals of design. Van de Velde had already broken the tradition of the Beaux-Arts-inspired *atelier*, replacing it with what he termed a 'workshop', something more along the lines of today's studio. The *Vorkurs* method expanded this theme and put the Bauhaus program in opposition to the French academy. The six-month course encapsulated all the aims of the school as a whole.

Half of the allocated time in the Bauhaus foundation course was spent crafting things like models. After 1923, Bauhaus innovation included partnership with industry, providing research and development as a means to offset costs. Product design at the Bauhaus centred on prototype development – new teapots, light fixtures, chairs – and much of this work was done in models. This industrial practice of creating scale models as part of product design was

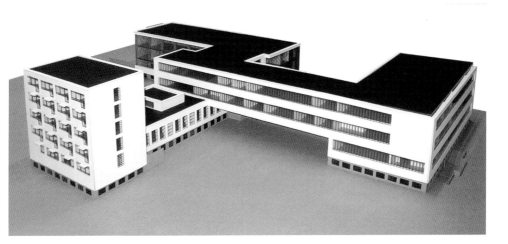

applied to architecture as a matter of course. Lastly, there was the concept of the model as offered by Itten as a vehicle for pure creativity. This type of model hovered between the sculptural and the architectural, much like the *Prouns* of El Lissitzky who urged, *"Don't read! Take paper, blocks, wood pieces; build, paint, construct!"* [11]

Taking over from Itten in 1923 was Hungarian László Moholy-Nagy, who strengthened Constructivist themes in the foundation course. The school was compelled to move to Dessau, allowing Gropius to design a purpose built facility featuring many Bauhaus innovations. It was in the new building, in 1927, that a separate department of architecture was properly formed, only a year before Gropius's departure. His replacement, Swiss architect Hannes Meyer, supported the new architecture department above all else, naming Ludwig Hilberseimer to head it. Ludwig Mies van der Rohe took over in 1930 and managed to make the Bauhaus first and foremost an architecture school. Growing National Socialist influence closed the school there, so Mies moved the Bauhaus to Berlin, as a private school, but even this was forced to close in 1933. Fourteen short years in total then, and many of these clouded by transition, yet the Bauhaus is cited at the most important design school of the twentieth century. [12] Most of that fame is owed to the *Vorkurs* and its two- and three-dimensional output: graphic work, product design and models.

Arguably, its fame and influence would not have been so great had it not been for its hostile closure by Nazi authorities. The resulting Bauhaus diaspora led to a well-documented dissemination of Bauhaus methods to a larger world. True, certain European and American critics had followed the progress of the Bauhaus from early on, but the school's continued influence is in large part due to the resettlement of its faculty. In 1937 Gropius went to Harvard, eventually bringing Marcel Breuer with him, and Mies became dean of a new architecture school at the Armour Institute, later to become the Illinois Institute of Technology.

Philip Johnson worked tirelessly in his capacity as director of the Department of Architecture at the Museum of Modern Art in New York to promote Mies and the Bauhaus in the USA through exhibitions and catalogues. Johnson had visited the Bauhaus in 1929 and was particularly impressed with the *Vorkurs*, *"a course in creative handwork, difficult to explain, but one of the most valuable courses at the Bauhaus."* [13] The impression of the model's status

within the range of Bauhaus output was enlarged by Johnson's inclusion of the faculty's private work side by side with that of the school. The pivotal 'Modern Architecture: International Exhibition' show at the MoMA – organised by Johnson, Hitchcock and Barr – ran in early 1932. A centrepiece of the exhibition was a detailed model of the Dessau Bauhaus. Mies was prominently featured in the catalogue, *The International Style* (Johnson's term), which described his skyscraper and office building projects realised thus far only as models.

When the Bauhaus closed Johnson assisted Josef and Anni Albers, securing them positions at the Black Mountain College in North Carolina, which functioned as a Bauhaus-in-exile, *"a spiritual heir and centre for the transmission of Bauhaus idea"*.[14] Josef Albers' Bauhaus design lab had from the start focused on paper designs, structural transformations with folding and cutting resulting in freeform sculpture, structures and models. It was the triangle of Harvard, IIT and Black Mountain that maintained Bauhaus academic influence in the States and not the short-lived New Bauhaus in Chicago. Lasting influence would not be achieved overnight, but the resettlement of the faculty and the interaction between Bauhaus-staffed institutions and other university programmes would lead to gradual adoption of *Vorkurs* methods, including modelling, by many schools of architecture in the years to come.

> *Although his [Gropius's] views were undoubtedly influential in some parts of Europe, they were to find an extraordinarily sympathetic and enthusiastic audience in his newly adopted country; so much so that by 1947, ten years after his arrival in Cambridge, the transplanted Bauhaus program had overtaken, not to say supplanted, the academy as the dominant force in American architectural design studios.*[15]

After the war the GI Bill swelled the numbers of most schools and the group dynamic of the *Vorkurs* was an effective means to cope with the jump in student numbers in the USA; similar changes were afoot in Europe with the foundation of so many polytechnical schools. *"The peculiar nature of the work of the École was ostensibly the grounds for protest by the* founding fathers of the Modern Movement: for instance Le Corbusier's response to the invitation to teach at the École des Beaux-Arts was to say that the whole institution should be razed to the ground and salt sprinkled on the site as a ritual of purification!"[16] Americans, it might be said, appreciated the hands-on approach of the *Vorkurs* and viewed models as democratic objects. Models as prototypes also appealed to preoccupations with research and development and courting industrial benefactors.

Despite this, Bauhaus or Modernist influence on American architecture schools in the 1940s and 1950s was fragmentary.[17] Where modelling might be accepted as an element of a revamped freshmen course, most schools still maintained a Beaux-Arts system of sorts for later studios:

> Two predominantly European educational models – the rigorous but rapidly receding Ecole des Beaux-Arts model of the American academy, and Walter Gropius's assimilated version of the Bauhaus program – were uncomfortably lodged alongside that of a third, homegrown American school, a blend of regionalism and pragmatism. In the best circumstances, this odd combination might resemble a kind of carefully balanced American Shinto; in the worst cases, it would display symptoms of an advanced state of academic schizophrenia.[18]

Even in the 1960s modelling was still not commonplace at many universities; it was treated as an alternative method among others. Most students provided models as ancillary information for final projects, but these were rather clumsy site models (showing a building in a landscape) or technical detail models revealing novel structural solutions. The highly crafted scale model carrying the bulk of an architectural idea and generated throughout the design process was still a rarity. The professional office increasingly made presentation models for client approval and competitions, but these were considered a luxury item.

Some of this began to change in 1969 with another exhibition at the MoMA, curated again by Philip Johnson. 'The New York Five' – Peter Eisenman, Michael Graves, Charles Gwathmey, John Hejduk and Richard Meier – were handpicked by Johnson as the next big thing. The exhibition was broadly successful and the resulting book, *Five Architects* published in 1975, even more so in terms of dissemination and reach. Johnson appreciated the strain of Modernism obvious in all the work (some of which had been touched by Bauhaus-minded mentors) and delighted in the projects' visual quality, something he had done with his 'Modern Architecture' show some thirty-seven years previously.

Despite the span of years separating the two shows, Johnson's vision remained constant. He promoted Modernism above all else on visual grounds and seemed to relish, as a curator, models in a gallery setting. The year after *Five Architects* was published Eisenman organised (with Johnson's blessing) 'Idea as Model' as part of the Institute for Architecture and Urban Studies, the first exhibition solely devoted to the scale model as an index of process and a site for theoretical inquiry. In the thirty or so years since, Johnson's so-called kids and their 'kids' have pushed the model in new directions linked by Bauhaus origin.

Sadar Vuga Arhitekti

Jurij Sadar and Bostjan Vuga

House D, Velenje, Slovenia   2003

A young and dynamic firm, Sadar Vuga introduces new forms and technologically savvy details to Slovenia and beyond. One of the principle ways they arrive at innovative architectural solutions is through aggressive modelling both in analogue and digital formats. With House D, a private suburban residence, sketch models hint at the possibility of treating the facades of the house as distinct bands or ribbons. A by-product of working with strips of paper in initial stages of design, these five bands or 'construction strips' are subsequently developed as each being materially different; some opaque, some translucent, some transparent.

Further definition of the bands introduced interesting tectonic possibilities at both vertical and horizontal edges and corners. What had been an effect of folding paper becomes the material and structural focus of the building envelope design which, in turn, helps to define the overall form of the building. Certain bands might continuously form a wall, a roof plane, an internal screen and floor plane, perhaps resembling a letter 'D' in section.

Paper and card models start to colour code based on materials and thematic choices; these are then worked up into more refined wood models that start to show resolution of the layers and folds of the bands. The site stitches into model investigations early as the house enjoys very different views on each side. The diversity of four house fronts extend into recognisable 'micro-ambients' which give the house its identity. As a system, the bands can respond to each view, the corners taking the formal transition from one elevation composition to the next.

Midway through the project's development, the model is recreated on the computer along with the site. Not only does this transfer easy access to calculated surface areas per band, but the computer also renders accurate perspectives for each approach to the building (the car versus the pedestrian, the neighbour versus the milkman). These become cinematic vignettes for the architects to study. The saturated pinks and greens of the virtual model are intentional; even the 'hardscapes' of the garden and the driveway are meant to be painted and form part of the reading of the bands.

Not only is the house banded in terms of facade: there is also a spatial banding of rooted entrance plinth to floating public rooms and to the

Opposite
This digital sketch model removes the site and concentrates on the short section of the house

Architecture and the Miniature

Right
A later stage process model in foam, which mimics the thickness of the intended building shell. The site, similarly rendered, is essential even at the early stages of the design

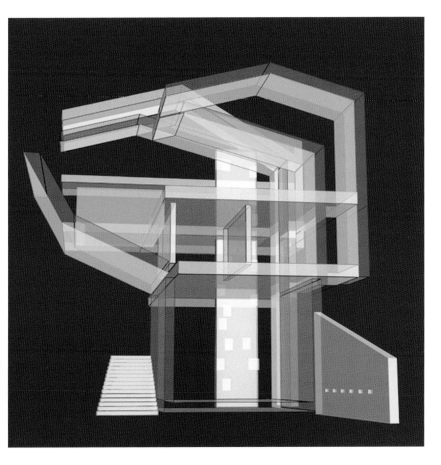

Opposite

A more refined analogue model iteration suggesting materials and treatment of glass panels on the court-yard facades. The shadow cast under the house adds to the illusion that House D is floating down the hillside

Below

A collage of digital model and sky, photographed roadside and background. The image situates the house more fully in the landscape, but the house itself loses something of its hovering quality seen elsewhere

Below

Finalised digital model experi-menting with textures, colour range and accurate reflections captured by the fenestration

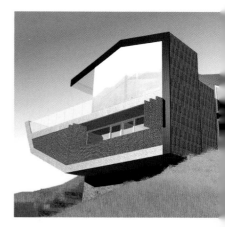

Architecture and the Miniature

pool with a view to the mountains. A simple motif suggested by sketch models in a rather perfunctory way comes to operate as a theme for the house – its skin, space and orientation of views. The digital model takes the baton where physical models stop short, offering a cinematic simulation of approach and sequence inside and out. Model types are used strategically, depending on the stage of development and the problem being addressed. It is worth noting that for Sadar Vuga all the model types they employ are working models, even the digital, none rests as the definitive final model.

Their computer models function differently to their physical models, and scale shifts within a range depending on the type of question asked of any given model. That said, none of their models for House D are fragmentary; each includes the whole of the house proposal, if not the landscape as well. This partly springs from the function of the bands to encapsulate all requirements of the house at once. Furthermore, the size of the house (250 square metres) is such that the building can more easily be represented whole per stage than, say, a civic building like Sadar Vuga's Chamber of Commerce and Industry in Ljubljana.

Opposite bottom
Shadows rake the interior to create a dynamic graphic *(left)*, with the background mountains added from site photographs. It is the obligatory poolside view *(far left)*, however, that actually reveals more about the interior of the house than any other image

Brian Bowman

Design for a House of under 2000 square feet   2003

An unorthodox studio assignment organised by assistant professor Pamela Unwin-Barkley, the project involved two phases of modelling. In phase one the students were asked to intensely study a given house design. This study included modelling the precedent building to a set scale (one-eighth), in a limited palette of materials. The level of craft expected was particularly fine and some students used the laser cutter to achieve this. Site models, by contrast, were treated simply, most often in cardboard, and focused only on topography. The house models had to reveal interiors which were as carefully constructed as the exterior. No figures, no furniture, no finishes beyond those suggested by the architecture were permitted.

Phase two involved designing a new house based on themes extracted from the precedent study. Normally, in school, a series of precedents are raided for ideas that may or may not be grafted into a final new design. Precedent study usually functions as a mode of preliminary research (pre-sketch model), almost entirely visual, that promises the new project will claim some meaningful context in terms of current practice or architectural history. Often this kind of research prompts anxiety in students who – before they even begin the project in earnest – are faced with the task of *"emulating but not copying"* so many notable examples. In the best circumstances precedent studies work as a loose meditation on a future project, seeing what themes represented by the examples stick. The unreasonable goal of this brand of precedent research is to magically distil the essence of the best designs of a type (in this example, a house of under 2000 square feet) and produce a coherent, original (yet historically/critically linked) architectural design.

Refusing this use of precedent, Unwin-Barkley strove to edit the process allowing the students to focus on a single work over a longer period of time in order to clearly enunciate, both theoretically and formally, what aspects of the precedent they admired. What is more, students were allowed to hold as closely to their precedent in their own

Opposite
Brian Bowman's design for a house of under 2000 square feet. Bowman's first variation introduces an elevated terrace on which the house is placed at a subtle angle

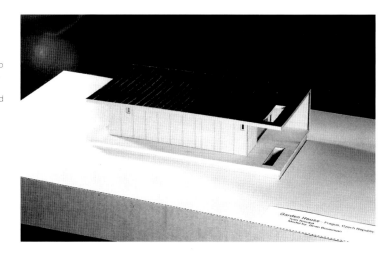

Below
Another variation, more inventive and complex, displayed as a model exploded axonometric. Here the vocabulary of the Kroupa house is elaborated and the student gains more control of his own design intentions

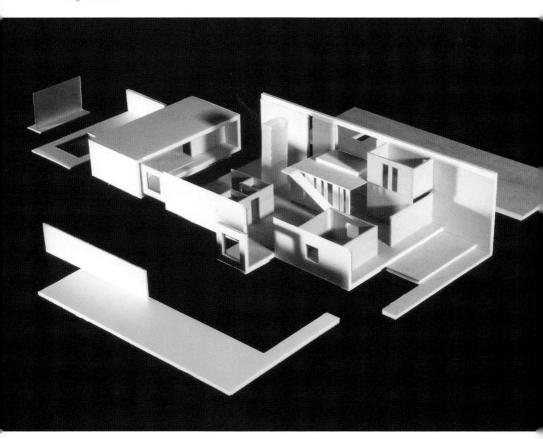

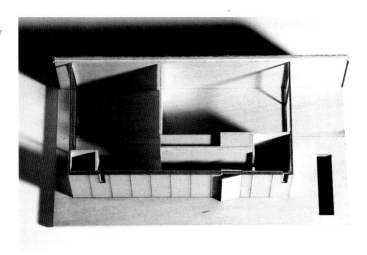

Right
Careful treatment of the interior
includes attention to service
spaces, even door swings

work as they wished. The faithful modelling of the precedent in phase one worked as a rehearsal for the design of phase two, which kept to the same scale and material. This design, in some cases, functioned as a variation on a given theme; a standard Beaux-Arts methodology applied to contemporary architecture. Most students, inculcated by a Modernist preconception that claims formal innovation is the sole barometer of creativity, struggled in finding balance between their precedent and their 'own' design for a house. Some felt they strayed too far from their precedent, others not enough. Judging the models side by side forced this sort of appraisal.

The point of both phases was to examine ways to improve small house design. The model assignment, however, triggered a wider debate on the topic of originality in architecture. By comparing the models, students and faculty could see precisely what the students valued in their precedent, what themes they elaborated upon and what aspects of the precedent they rejected as useful in their own work. What a third party might view as an exercise in sloppy copying became a turning point

in the education of Unwin-Barkley's students who admitted the project was the most difficult they had encountered.

A drawing exercise might, perhaps, have covered similar territory, but the models accomplished three things. First, the task of building a well-crafted model of the precedent house forced students to linger over a design much longer than they would ordinarily; the assignment made them look at someone else's work for as long as they typically looked at their own projects. Second, the spaces of these tightly packed houses were best visualised in model form. Third, themes that might not be easily verbalised could still be touched upon in the crafting of the model – much as Frank Lloyd Wright claimed to learn through his fingers.

UN Studio

Ben van Berkel and Caroline Bos

Mercedes-Benz Museum, Stuttgart, Germany 2001- 6

Physical models are indispensable when creating and representing complex spaces. UN Studio's design for the Mercedes-Benz Museum in Stuttgart is difficult to read in plan or section, but the idea for the building is broadcast clearly in a series of models. The museum is organised across six trefoil-shaped floors all linked by ramps; one might picture a triangulated Guggenheim Museum. Indeed, as with Wright's design, the exhibition sequence starts at the top and spirals down, but the van Berkel and Bos design is not so formally straightforward.

"Spatially, the building is structured as a double helix. The leaves of the trefoil rotate around a triangular void, forming six horizontal planes that alternately occupy single- and double-floor heights, resulting in six double-height and six single-height exhibition spaces. The organisation does not involve a continuous single surface; the six floor plates themselves are level, with gently sloping ramps bridging the height difference between them." [1]

This ambitious scheme also contains a number of shortcuts and moments for spatial 'cross-referencing'. Here, the body is also an automobile where the galleries also read as twisting and turning fragments of autobahn.

The project lingers over the geometry of the section and questions of circulation: things models are generally effective at tackling. Models for the museum included initial sketch models in paper, often marked with arrows or letters to keep track of the levels. The trefoil plates are there early on. A circulation model is built with pins and rubber laces. Different ramp options are then tried over the course of several more sketch models of paper and foam, programme filters in by stages zoning different plates.

Midway through the process, a digital model is created in order to generate simplified section models, produced by a rapid-prototyping machine, which can be used to accurately check ramp slopes, ceiling heights and whether spaces really might visually cross reference, which is to say, reveal vignettes experienced or yet to come in the intended circulation path. This plastic model receives a rough site model with abstracted cars, vegetation and figures.

Even at a much more refined stage another model is called for and at quite a generous scale. This model fills a studio and (like those famous models of St Peter's or St Paul's) is large enough for the designers and clients to inhabit! Such a thing is not put together for mere showmanship, the large model more effectively looks at issues such as quality of light, facade composition, the relationship between service cores and gallery space, oblique views across plates, and relationship to the ground plane.

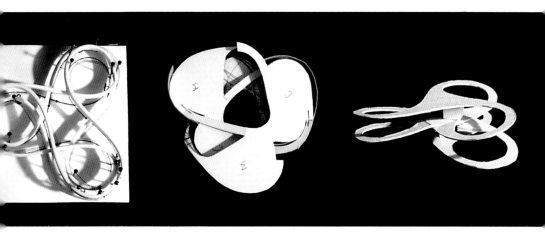

Above
Early sketch models target circulation and the resulting section

Below
A much larger scale model, still monochromatic, exploring sequence, section and space. The size of the model is such that one can stand in the atrium and view the whole project as a three-dimensional panorama

There is an element of showmanship, of course. A large model says to the client or planning committee: if the design can be realised and appreciated at this hefty scale, surely it can be built and do all we claim it can. The novelty of being able to bodily merge with the model, sense it as a container rather than just as an object and, yes, feel big in proportion to the project, is as much a novelty now as it was in Sangallo's or Wren's day.

In parallel with physical model development, a sophisticated digital version is developed, reacting to changes made in the physical model and prompting changes to the physical one at the same time. This virtual model will eventually include structural documentation and will work as the basis for construction drawings and virtual testing. In terms of representing the building, the virtual model can be rendered with accurate daylight and shadow and photomontaged into aerial and site photography.

Again, this signals how eminently buildable the project is. Good photomontages, like final models, suggest the building is, on some level, already manifested. They push the nose of the project just enough into the realm of the real world to demand ascent, while staying ideal enough to suggest the fantasy and to ask what if.

Below
Still a working model, this
version was rapidly prototyped
and set in a detailed site model
giving the proposal a sense of
scale and orientation

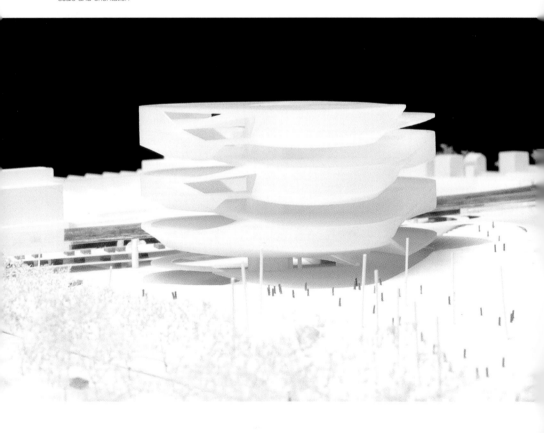

Architecture and the Miniature

Right
This second wave sketch model looks at ramp-way systems and establishes a central atrium affording views across the trefoil

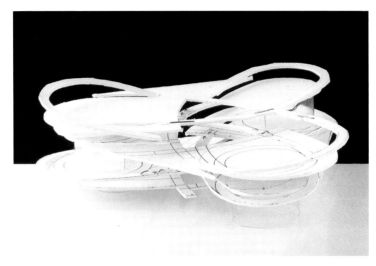

Right
Here programmatic zones represented in yellow foam start to stack as cylinders that traverse the section

Right
The section is exaggerated in this model, with coloured foam identifying basic programmatic relationships

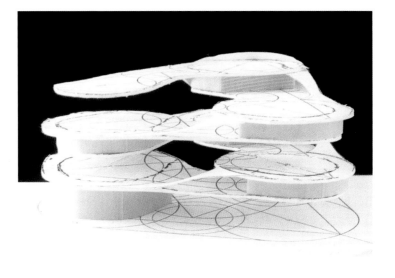

Sketch Models

Can models aid in overcoming designer's block? Demands for originality can sometimes be daunting. Not every architect has a vision of the whole of a project in a classic flash of inspiration. Diving into three dimensions right away, even in the loosest, least committed fashion, does not necessarily seem as natural as jumpstarting a design by doodling with a pen. Yet sketching in three dimensions, crafting a sketch model, can yield faster, fuller results than traditional sketching on a pad of paper. Some architects, perhaps owing to their training, admit that they do not think in three dimensions straight away; they prefer to create initially in plan, say. The truth of the matter is a lucid three-dimensional imagination is not required to work with sketch models. The sketch model can seem to do the thinking for you.

Sketch or process models are three-dimensional sketches, ideas made visible but not concluded in any way. They need not strain to arrive at a definitive model, but can be crafted for their own ends, separated from the goal of a final design. The relationship between process and final models is tricky. Not all final models are achieved through a succession of process models; in some cases final models are merely process models stopped at a critical point and polished. Being more elementary and essential, it might be assumed that process models have been around a long time. The fact is, however, that process models are relatively new. They were celebrated as part of the Modernist method but only recently became a sign of professional or avant-garde credentials.

Process models are almost always made by the hand of the designer and so claim the architect's touch and authorial aura. The same cannot be said for other types of models. Architects may trust their final presentation models to their staff or subcontracted professional model makers, but they do make their own process models. Yet the fact that most finished models are not crafted by their designer does not stop us from fantasising that all models have a tactile and direct link to the architect; in some sense, the authored process model legitimises all the others. Each process model being bespoke helps this assumption along;

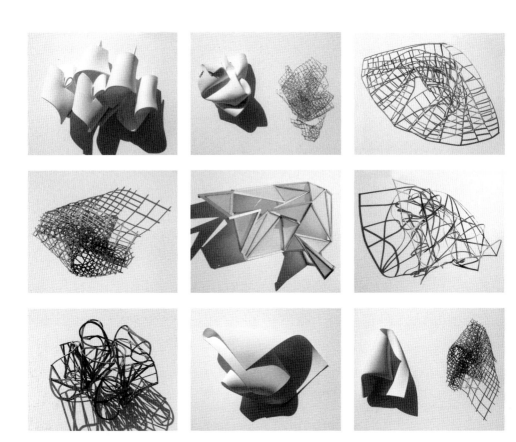

drawings can be photocopied or mechanically drafted, models (until recently) cannot. Then there is what might be called the 'Doubting Thomas Effect' of models generally, the desire not only to see a proposal but to verify it through touch. If individual drawings seem too abstract or notational, the model – even a cursory one – forgoes the guesswork associated with putting plans, sections and elevations together mentally:

> First, unlike other miniatures, architectural models belong to that pragmatic stage in a building's evolution when the model, or maquette, evokes the not-yet-constructed edifice, an ideal edifice one day to be completed (pending the patron's approval of the model itself). Yet models are more than mere drawings, more than the two-dimensional blueprints from which buildings may be constructed by the expert but can hardly be imagined by the layman. Architectural models are already a significant step towards the realisation of the final product, a step in the process of desire beyond the drawing and into a more than conceptual space.[1]

Important as they are, process models are of primary interest to architectural education and a fringe of the profession – albeit a fringe consisting, it would appear, of the more famous offices. Such objects are nearly impossible to conserve and their lives are usually brief. For any process to be effective, it must eventually end. From the napkin sketch to the project deadline,

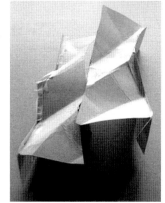

Right
José Oubrerie design team, sketch models for the Museum of Ethnography, Geneva, Switzerland, 1997. The design for the museum was conceived as a braid of three volumes that rise in section across the site. Before initial drawings or digital visualisations could be undertaken, a series of rough models in paper was assembled to conceptualise the braid before truly representing it

Opposite
Second-year model assignment. Assistant Professor Chris Beorkrem asks students to create a gestural model in coated Funky Foam sheeting and then translate it in other media, prompting basic considerations of structure, profile and geometry. Models made by (from top row, left to right) Gillard Yau, Vershae Crawley, Tiffany Johnson, Anna Struthers Alison Price, Lee Waller, Gilard Yau, Christopher Campbell and Anna Struthers.

process is bracketed. Stoppage permits other model types to emerge, models not completely bound to their own making and not necessarily tied to their authorial hand.

The School Crit

Architects start projects in different ways. Some begin with a series of sketches, others may start in plan or in section or elevation. Still others might start with painting (Hadid) or photography, while some might begin a project with text (Hejduk). Then there are those who begin with a rough model (Gehry). Process models favour journey over destination. They are trophies of design work – proof of time, consideration and the testing of ideas. Such models testify to the evolution of a project and the merits of trial and error. This is in contrast to romantic notions of the work arriving in a flash of insight and being expressed perfectly the first time. The process or sketch model is quick and gestural.

Drawing and modelling can work in parallel, with napkin sketches being easily translated into sketch models. Such models can serve as notation, where the pieces of the model are not meant to read as architectonic forms but as other information – when modelling ideas about circulation, for example. As snapshots of the design process, such models may be more useful as an archive (they are presented as a collection) than as just a heuristic device. This archive can be raided at any stage of the design process and used as a formal palette for subsequent work. *"Perpetual change would pass before us without deadlines and in perpetual monotony. If representation did not possess the obscure power of making a past impression present once more, then no impression would ever appear as either similar or dissimilar from a previous one."* [2]

Most models seen in schools of architecture are process models, models created in an effort to arrive at a project. They can be grouped together as seeming unfinished, fragmentary, serial and materially slipshod. Such models are typically presented at the end of semester in the sequence in which they were crafted, as part of the review critique. They function, along with drawings, computer renderings and other modes of research, as ways for the student to outline the biography of a design; and, by extension, the autobiography of the designer. The project's evolution illustrated by sketches and models stands in for the project as a whole. The final set of drawings and model are rarely judged alone, or never seem quite satisfactory, and this results in a retreat into process. As this kind of presentation amounts to an accepted ritual in school, it could be said that academic projects are not judged solely on the merits of a last iteration, but as a collection of false starts or stabs at solving a problem. This would not have been the case at the École des Beaux-Arts where an initial sketch *parti* would be approved within a set number of hours and a final set of drawings submitted. All intervening stages between the two went unacknowledged and the project was judged without its author present.

A project shown as a group of process models at an academic review forces internal comparison. Wider debate is forestalled by providing a self-regulating series, the contents of which all resemble each other in certain respects, but never replicate each other exactly. This tactic encourages an estimation of resemblance within a set, rather than a formal assessment of a definitive model. If a defining factor of a beautiful thing is its totality then process models cannot be said to be beautiful as none of them approaches totality; indeed they avoid it. These models are part of the creative process, they function not to represent foregone conclusions about a project but to express emerging ideas as yet unsettled in regard to the project as a whole. They are handled quickly, like a sketch, in order to capture a fleeting thought; Frank Gehry times his at 3.4 minutes on average. [3] Time is a primary factor of process models, their numbers boast a material manifestation of work and thinking done in a span of time, their seriality implies temporality. The model must work through time proportionally as if the model were a small-scale building requiring a proportional span of time to render itself. Process models are not just academic; they remain an infrequent but important part of practice. Frank Gehry exemplifies this approach using process models at the fulcrum of his practice and teaching.

Architectural design processes may flow from (1) mental exercises, turning something over in the mind's eye, to (2) sketching and drawing not detailed plans, elevations or sections but evocative notations for future work and (3) modelling. In terms of process all three

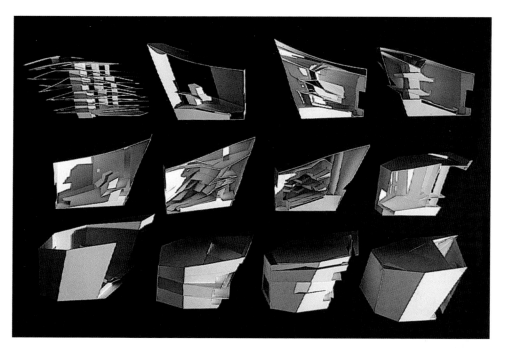

Above and right

Zaha Hadid Architects, Cardiff Bay Opera House, Cardiff, Wales, 1994. These investigations of the auditorium are sketch models of a high order. Serial, evocative, checking different spatial and formal options, these models are research. The forms would seem to vacillate within some predetermined envelope and adhere to an architectural language even at early stages. There is a visual power to the grouping, an insight into a creative process

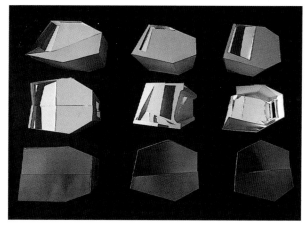

Opposite

UN Studio, Ponte Parodi, Genoa, Italy 2001. UN Studio's winning design for a 23,000 sq m pier-piazza in the city's harbour began with a kinetic sketch model of interconnected cubes. Manipulation of the sketch model suggested a *parti* of angled plates and interstitial voids that still adhered to the rectangular site on the water. The model was digitally refined early on in the process, but the genesis of the overall form required taped bits of paper and tugging hands.

Left and below
Craig Bethel, design for a
bicycle shop, 2005. Using a
special paper, this student
created a sketch model that
exceeds standard expec-
tations. Still gestural and
ambiguous in terms of scale,
the model clearly broadcasts
the overall intention for the
project. Lacy interior volumes
intersect and bend just as the
stretchable mesh does

Architecture and the Miniature

modes are working the same territory. Conceptualising, sketching and modelling are all ways of thinking about an architectural problem without necessarily arriving at a stable conclusion. Process models can be heuristic devices, tools to arrive at an idea, objects that allow for invention at a project's earliest stages. Models need not represent a whole building, nor do they need to be precise or at a consistent scale. Process models can render invisible flows like circulation, memory traces, arbitrary geometrical manoeuvres. A model built to explore an aspect of a project at one scale may be seized upon as the solution to the whole in another. Modelling with scraps and scissors brings the process model closer to, but never quite to the point, where the model mimics actual building on some essential level. They are reductive, abstract and target single themes: structure, space, light, movement.

One of the true delights of the sketch model has to do with its misreading. A model crafted for one project might be turned upside down and reinterpreted for another. Sketch models of various scales made for different purposes might be thrown together as a three-dimensional collage suggesting something new. Because they are quick and cheap, sketch models lend themselves to this kind of material and conceptual recycling. Such free-wheeling form making may unnerve or annoy those used to working in more methodical ways, even during the early stages of a project. The sketch model may not suit everyone, but it is worth noting other reasons architects might avoid this way of exercising their creativity.

Child's Play

"What if themes of architectural modernism at the beginning of the twentieth century had been absorbed, refracted, and reassembled within a theory of cultural modernity in which children and toys played a leading role, a theory that continues to illuminate the problematics of culture at the end of the century?" [4] Detlef Mertins posed this question in the first lines of the catalogue for the 1993 'Toys and the Modernist Tradition' exhibition. The answer largely came in Norman Brosterman's 1997 *Inventing Kindergarten* where he asserted Modernism's unacknowledged debt to a new early education curriculum:

> *The Victorian childhood of the seminal modernists and their audience at large coincided with the development and widespread embrace of a radical educational system that was a catalyst in exploding the cultural past and restructuring the resulting intellectual panoply with a new worldview. It was never fodder for argument over absinthe and Gauloises in Montmartre cafés, nor was it taught at tradition-bound academies. It has been largely ignored because its participants – three- to seven-year-olds – were in the primary band of the scholastic spectrum. It was the seed pearl of the modern era and it was called kindergarten.* [5]

Kindergarten was founded by Friedrich Wilhelm August Froebel, born and raised near Weimar, later home to the original Bauhaus. Intending to be an architect, Froebel took interest in elementary education, studying Pestalozzi, [6] whose methods and Rousseau-inspired critiques [7] later directly influenced the Bauhaus manifesto. Froebel incorporated his own interest in crystallography, postulating that the same laws evidenced by the geometric formations of crystals governed the growth of children and society in general. *"Manipulating models of these forms correctly would reveal and illuminate the logic of creation."* [8] Froebel brought this new education to very young students in an effort to tap the genius of the

young, *"the free republic of childhood"*. His colleagues organised schools across Germany and Switzerland. Froebel developed and standardised his 'object lessons' as Kindergarten Gifts. These included drawing, paper folding and cutting exercises, building block assignments, modelling with clay and sticks.[9]

Brosterman states that Le Corbusier, Paul Klee, Walter Gropius, Josef Albers, Wassily Kandinsky, Johannes Itten, Piet Mondrian, Theo van Doesburg, George Vantongerloo, Gerrit Rietveld, Georges Braque and Frank Lloyd Wright all experienced some form of Kindergarten. Evidence is scant, but Le Corbusier, Itten and Wright certainly did have some contact with Kindergarten. Itten was a trained primary schoolmaster in Froebelian methodology.

Before Frank Lloyd Wright was born his mother claimed she instinctively knew she would give birth to a great architect. She decorated the nursery with images of famous buildings and encouraged baby Frank to play with special building blocks, purchased at a Universal Exhibition pavilion showcasing a new German teaching method for the very young called Kindergarten.[10] Wright would relate in his memoirs how so much of his talent sprung from this special toy.[11] *"The smooth shapely maple blocks with which to build, the sense of which never afterward leaves the fingers: so form became feeling. These primary forms were the secrets of all effects ... which ever got into the architecture of the world."*[12] Froebel blocks were introduced to the first Kindergartens in the early nineteenth century as one of the Gifts.

The watering down of the original Kindergarten in subsequent decades is well documented. A trace of the Gifts, however, can still be seen in, for example, Montessori education. But the real successor to Froebel's Kindergarten is not found with the under-fives.

Architecture and the Miniature

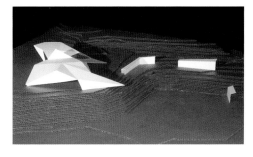

Above and left

Tim Lucci, design for a bicycle shop, 2005. With a simple site model of corrugated cardboard, this sketch model of folded paper can negotiate topography from the start of the process. The structure of the paper itself, creases and cuts, starts to suggest a notional tectonic language to be elaborated later. The bike shelters detached in the landscape, though small, suggest the project is not seen as a pure autonomous object, but a series of fragments that acknowledge the landscape even in an abbreviated representation.

Rather, object lesson Kindergarten can be seen to have flourished at university level in schools of architecture. Brosterman never makes this point, but his survey would support the case that Johannes Itten brought Kindergarten methods to the Bauhaus *Vorkurs* and, blending them with aspects of Surrealism and De Stijl, offered Kindergarten to aspiring architects. Architecture school is the true successor of Kindergarten.

Well before architecture school or even grammar school, one has been exposed to models and the concept of the miniature as an object of leisure and pedagogy folded into structured play. That sense of play re-emerges in architecture school. The equation imagination = play = the creative act has a respectable pedigree, commencing with Freud's conclusion that *"the opposite of play is not what is serious but what is real"*.[13] Josef Albers, describing the preliminary course in 1928, explained, *"inventive construction and pioneering observation are developed – at least in the beginning – through undisturbed and uninfluenced, that is unprejudiced experimentation which, at first, amounts to aimless playing with material"*.[14]

Romantic theories of art, like those of Friedrich von Schiller, acknowledged that play was essential to creativity. Schiller argued that the Play Drive (*Spieltrieb*) synthesised the material and formal into an ultimate beauty and art intended to educate. What could better exemplify synthesis of material and form through play than the sketch model?

José Oubrerie

French Cultural Centre, Damascus, Syria   1980 - 2

Nurtured early in his career under Le Corbusier's tutelage, José Oubrerie brings a unique model-making approach to projects ranging from private houses to institutional buildings such as the French Cultural Centre in Damascus. Most of Oubrerie's work could be said to be modelcentric. This is not to say he avoids drawing, quite the contrary, but for Oubrerie drawings run in parallel with a whole series of 'research models'. Research begins with several sketch models. These are typically folded, crumpled or sliced pieces of paper. These objects are evocative, fragmentary, evanescent. They are fashioned too quickly to even permit glue to dry, so they are often taped or stapled and photographed before a slight breeze might undo them. Once these sketch models suggest a direction, slightly more refined models are built with some semblance of scale and indication of site conditions. Already at this stage, orientation and light effects are checked by model.

Broken by phases of drawing (particularly sections), more advanced models elaborate interior spaces, key details and connection to site, but these are still mostly of cardstock and constantly revised. Indeed, Oubrerie does not hesitate to revisit abandoned models or reorient, merge and heavily edit others. No model is precious, all are in service to the evolving idea for the building. Three-quarters of the way through the process, drawings

are used to resolve inconsistencies or examine potential suggested by the models. Elevations are considered at this relatively late stage, conceived as the result of plan and section. These drawings are then used as templates for a definitive model, usually made in wood. This model, in turn, then serves as a template which could help revise a final set of drawings. Depending on the project, the final model might come apart to reveal the section and notable aspects of the interior.

Oubrerie does introduce the computer to study interior and exterior perspectives, check specific daylighting questions depending on the building's location and so on. In short, the computer is used for those things his physical models either cannot do or not do so well. For instance, the computer model might render what elements of the site are reflected in a pane of glass on the facade from a given angle. But, for Oubrerie, the design process is rooted in working in three touchable dimensions, with the aim to sculpt space at any scale.

With the French Cultural Centre he started with basic research, a 'premonitory sketch' and a conceptual model in folded paper. Given the tight site (15 x 22 metres), more models were built to resolve competing ambitions for dynamic space and programmatic fit. A theatre, offices and support spaces float above a lobby and gallery, while a roof garden captures views of the city. Having

Right

An early sketch model (sketchier than most) looking at the auditorium placement and exploring possible routes from the auditorium to the lower lobby

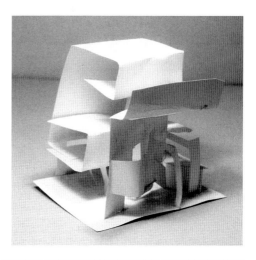

Below

A middle-stage model in museum board reveals the nesting of served and service spaces in section. The design has not fundamentally diverged from themes established in the first paper and tape sketch models, yet a whole series of pragmatic issues has been attended to

Left
A quick sketch model grappling with a long list of programmatic requirements and a relatively tight site footprint. The model shows José Oubrerie's initial thoughts on how to layer space and hang volumes, working from the top down

established a complex section, further models start to target facades. Working with paper again, a continuous plane is designed to wrap the theatre and then become part of the elevation. Circulation had to be carefully considered given the position of the theatre. A catwalk links the upper spaces, while an ingenious 'Leonardo da Vinci' stair allows for an internal and external staircase to exist in the same space in plan, also becoming an interesting formal element in the overall scheme.

A final model in wood was built in parallel with a set of drawings, each informing the other over the span of their development. Indeed, this model was *"not initially conceived as a presentation model, but as crucial to the elaboration of the design"*. This model also helped government officials and local contractors understand the design inside and out. The cultural centre is an impossible object, full of programme yet also full of grand spaces. This quality was achieved by intense modelling, working out proximities and circulation in section rather than plan and deploying architectural tricks like the doubled stair in an effort to conserve valuable space for better effect.

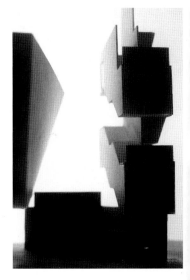

Above
This model study of the vertical circulation tests Oubrerie's hope to fuse a ceremonial open staircase with a required concealed fire stair, one wraps around the other and takes no additional space in plan

Left and above
The final model for the cultural centre in wood. Elevations are refined after the section and plan, these elaborate the interior disposition of spaces and functions. A generous roof garden is featured, catching breezes and framing views of Damascus

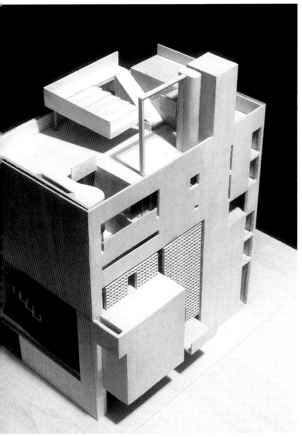

Frank O Gehry

Gehry Partners

Walt Disney Concert Hall, Los Angeles, California, USA 1999-2003

This series of early studies for the Walt Disney Concert Hall appeals to a concept of process: they announce before any subsequent image that the work to follow is world-class, avant-garde and formally challenging because the biography of their architecture starts with roughly assembled models. This notion of process is necessarily tied to a question of origin. For Frank Gehry, these types of models coincide with his trademark valorisation of his initial 'napkin sketch'. The key to a Gehry project is to trace its manifestation as a building back to original sketches and models and find the latter in the former as a kind of proof of genius.

In many ways his success has hinged on his fidelity to initial impressions. *"It looks like we are tearing up paper to make models, and I just roll up the paper and throw it all out. It is not like that. It is much more precise and careful. We work from the inside out, mostly."*[1] He describes the task of making such models in endless succession and keeping track of them: *"It takes a long time. It is like watching paint dry, and I will move things. Sometimes it goes too far and then we pull it back. That is why we have such a neat archive, because when* *we're in the heat of it, we'll record changes on a daily basis, because I know that I go too far and I want to go back and recall things, so we can rebuild."*[2] The project is not represented or documented by the process, the project is the process, it springs from model investigations one piece of folded paper at a time.

The indexical display, models pinned to a neutral field, provides a retrospective taxonomy, a field of what ifs. Like a butterfly collection, the display shows different species of designs, some extinct, some merely the forbears for subsequent iterations. Pulled together as a genealogy, resemblance keeps them organised as an ensemble, but it is difficult to trace a direct sequence or chronology. Given the eventual form of the exterior of the concert hall, these early studies of the audiorium itself seem rather muted. Even so, there is a surprising range to these models. The grouping, the collection, is not a set of variations on a theme, but several themes brought to a level of finish sufficient to tell them all clearly apart.

It would be wrong to paint Gehry's modelling as purely intuitive. What the concert hall series shows is that he carefully studies programme and typology and then creates conditions, framed by that research, in which to model. Within those parameters a certain breed of form making takes place, guided by research of another order, a sculptural one, an interest in surface and formal

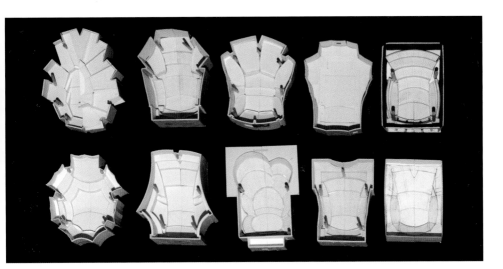

juxtaposition. What might be thought of as his signature manipulations are really only a part of a wider practice grounded in the mundane: budget programme and winning client approval.

Perhaps too much has been made of his office's use of CATIA (computer-aided three-dimensional interactive application) technology as if it mitigates unorthodox designs by digitally translating complex geometries into a format friendly to structural engineers and contractors. CATIA does aid in drafting and construction; it is also a design tool in its own right, but its functionality does not economise the design process so much as the manifestation of the design, which for Gehry still originates in the analogue model. The excuse that the architect cannot learn the new technology and so is bound to working with paper is really an excuse to conserve features of the analogue not easily replicated elsewhere.

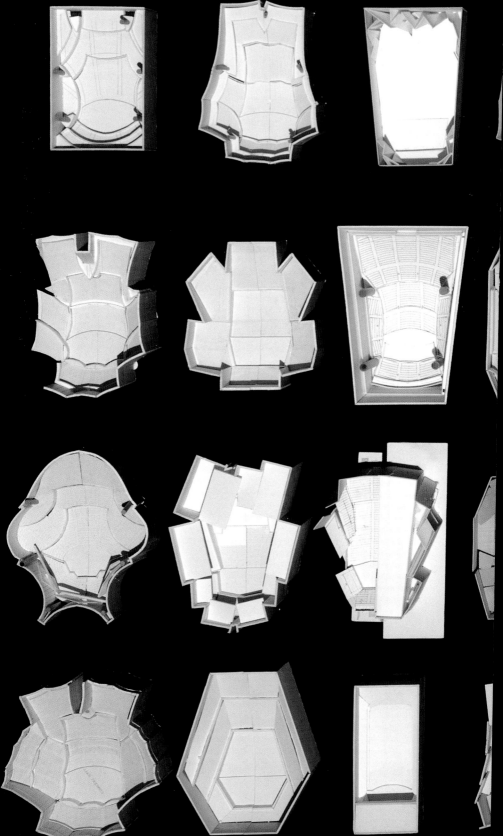

Left

A further 20 digital study
models of the auditorium. The
series has its own charm and
reminds you that forms which
appear whimsical can be the
result of tedious research.
These models, a step beyond
the sketch, are used to work
through design questions.
Until the form is realised at this
level, it cannot be evaluated
or folded into subsequent
research

Le Corbusier and José Oubrerie

Church of Saint-Pierre de Firminy, Firminy-Vert, France
1960-2005

The last project of Le Corbusier was a church design for the town of Firminy in the Auvergne. Assisted by José Oubrerie, Le Corbusier made a series of site studies, sketches and early models in advance of the official commission in 1960. Subsequent to the commission, more studies were made including several models, some in paper, others in wood, of a conical structure rising from the Jura plain as a kind of mountain. Various fragmentary models were made of the cone's base, facades and interiors trying radically different options. The scheme was largely completed in 1962, Le Corbusier died in 1965. Yet the project for St-Pierre de Firminy went forward and construction began in 1970, helped along by Oubrerie and practised members of Le Corbusier's atelier. Shortly thereafter local elections changed the political scene, the building of the church was halted along with the intended construction of two more Unité housing blocks. Only the foundation and base walls of the church were completed.

The project languished for three decades owing to continued political and financial turmoil. Critics noted the lost opportunity this presented: *"The Church of St Pierre in Firminy-Vert was Le Corbusier's last building, and could be seen as an architectural form of musical coda, the striking finale to a vast array of works."*[1] When, in the mid-1980s, there was a move to place a gymnasium on the site, an argument erupted returning to the question of the church. It was decided a competition could be held for a new church design, but a case was made that the previous design was still a going concern in the person of Oubrerie and in the approved drawings and models of Le Corbusier. The confusion was settled when not only the archive material from the late 1950s and early 1960s was produced, but also more drawings and models of the church – made by Oubrerie in the intervening years.

A large final model with a demountable facade revealed a finished interior in wood, with the added effect of numerous drilled holes in the cone itself bringing constellations to the interior. In the face of this archive of process, particularly the models, no one could deny the claims of the project. Had there been a competition, it would probably still have prevailed as a radical and challenging work given over two decades of refinement. Only now has its construction been restarted and Firminy can claim a new work by Le Corbusier nearly 40 years after his death. The church was conserved, cocoon-like, by the objects spun out of its own elaboration. The project survived intact on the strength of process models.[2]

Below
Le Corbusier and José
Oubrerie at work on the
Firminy model in the studio.
Drawings litter the table and
are revised with the model

Below
A final model in wood showing
the resolution of the entrance
ramp and its link to the landscape. The model can be
disassembled to provide views
of the interior

Below
Something like a final model
clarifies the innovative drainage
system, the inclusion of the
skylights and the editing of
the bell tower

Architecture and the Miniature

Right

The design from start to finish, spanning decades, includes constituent elements: a large mountain-like volume, elevated base, bell tower and entrance ramp. Recombinations of these elements and changes to profile and proportion pre-occupy much of the process

Right

Another early model for the church with a slender profile of a conic projection that moves from a round to a square volume at the base. Different sun blocks are tried, including a plane cut with irregular cave-like holes. The site is also modelled with a hint of the nearby foothills

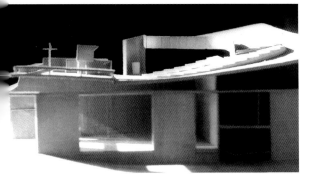

Left

The base, modelled on its own, houses offices, library and a smaller chapel. Visible on top is the ramping floor of the church

Left

A further investigation of the base sees the refinement of the altar space and stepped cascade of the floor area intended for chairs

NOX   Lars Spuybroek assisted by Dave Lee
Centre Pompidou 2, Metz, France   2003

Dave Lee
Hayden Planetarium Thesis Project, New York, New York,
USA   2002

A benefit of the scalar gap offered by conventional modelling is found in the use of heuristic devices. The Rotterdam office of NOX, headed by Lars Spuybroek, conceptualised a large building design with a composition of balloons lassoed with rubber straps. Part programmatic analysis, part formal invention, the balloon model took advantage of scale, playing on the notion of the bubble diagram as a spatial as well as an organisational tool. The straps hold the balloons in place and approximate a polygonal mesh, each strap a spline, defined by the composition of the whole. Each intersection of the straps was tagged, becoming a point of reference in a subsequent computer model.

A competition for a cultural complex in Metz, the programme included a large exhibition hall, black box theatre, auditorium, café, shops and an adjacent public square meant to merge with the building not unlike the scheme for the Centre Pompidou in Paris. Rather than ape the iconic grid of the Beaubourg, Spuybroek, assisted by Dave Lee, introduced a new geometry that would likewise subdivide the spaces of the complex and provide for architectural continuity throughout. This geometry itself is spatial, the voids found between the balloons – a soap bubble matrix – capable of housing infrastructure. With this move,

the structural grid and exposed infrastructure of Richard Rogers and Renzo Piano are merged.

In truth, the balloon model was quickly built and quick to deteriorate; the balloons started to deflate within hours and the model had to be breathlessly fed into the computer by taking co-ordinate readings with a digital stylus. By necessity, the virtual model took over early on in the process and developed well beyond the scope suggested by the balloons, but the core ideas for the design were found and captured in the unorthodox sketch model. Interior renderings show the bubble matrix in all its cyber-Piranesian splendour. Even the exterior renderings clearly reference the straps of the original model, now gargantuan.

Such an unusual approach to modelling does not develop overnight. You can find hints of the Pompidou 2 modelling strategy in the graduate work of Lee who studied at Columbia University. While not using balloons, his thesis project employs similar forms and the characteristic straps, except that here the straps predominate. A design for the Hayden Planetarium at the Rose Center, part of the American Museum of Natural History, Lee's models are composed of clear vinyl straps pinned to a plaster core. The pins work just as the tags did in the project for Metz.

Below
This sketch model comprises
a composition of balloons,
and operates fully in the so-
called 'Gulliver Gap' by taking
advantage of the scale it
assumes versus the size of
everyday objects.

Below
An interior view of Centre
Pompidou 2, showing the
circulation and the section.
Despite the collage of photographs, this clearly remains
a model

Architecture and the Miniatu

Right
The curving lattice of voids
between the balloons is conceived as structure throughout
Pompidou 2

It is interesting to view such a model as a
struggle to reconcile the hand-crafted object with
a digital aesthetic. Lee's model seems a tactile
equivalent of a digital wire-frame model. Its attractiveness springs from its negotiation of both model
conditions. The materiality and scale of the model
are part of its visual charm. The vinyl reflects light
unevenly, the stamped letters on the ends of the
straps promise precision, the pins suggest an
architectural voodoo.

You might question how well such a model
communicates. The question then becomes, what
does it mean to represent? Whereas the digital
model for Pompidou 2 starts to answer questions
about intended skin and structure, spatial divisions
and quality of light, Lee's academic model appears
to reject digital translation because his aim was to
render materially the digital. You can imagine this
model was intended to be ambiguous, to suggest
tectonic conditions but not immediately resolve
them, reveal but not delineate potentials. This
sensibility is retained and refined in the later work
at NOX where the analogue model for Pompidou
2 does not receive as much visual polish, but
nonetheless suggests both formal and structural
aspects and channels potential for subsequent
digital work.

Opposite
After the balloon model has
been digitally translated, the
design process runs its course.
Here, an exterior view shows
resolution of the proposed
building's envelope, while the
figures denote scale

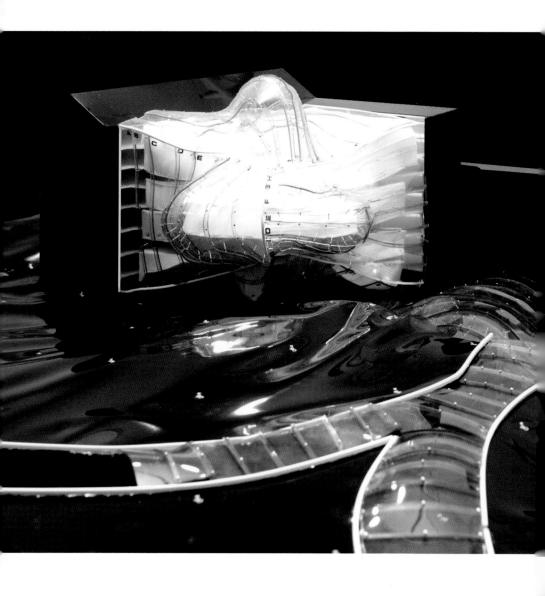

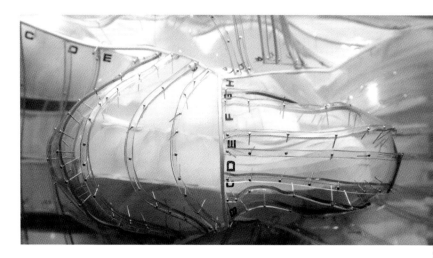

Above
A detail model of Dave Lee's Planetarium project, showing coded transparent vinyl straps and the evocative network of pins fastening the envelope to an inner core.

Left
A distinctive model language is shared by the planetarium proposal and the site, a hand-wrought liquid 'digitalscape'

Representational Modes

A model built. John Hejduk, the 'quiet one' of the New York Five, designed in 1973 a project that as a model has haunted the critical landscape ever since. His Wall House, also called the Bye House (designed for Cooper Union landscape architect Ed Bye), was a severe formal abstraction, eminently architectural and nearly uninhabitable. The project was part of a body of research launched earlier with 'Texas Rangers' Colin Rowe, Robert Slutzky and Bernard Hoesli – the culmination of their nine square studio assignment and Hejduk's own Diamond House series: projects grounded in the axonometric drawing and the model and completely new to the academic scene.

Philip Johnson remarks in his postscript to *Five Architects*: *"His 'wall' house could have (it never will be built) the eerie feeling of Hadrian at Tivoli or Mies' 1923 Brick House: endless wall with squiggles. Geometry again, but isolated, clear, simple. What would they look like at full scale?"* [1] The answer: not so good. In 2002 the project that would never be built was constructed posthumously on an improbable site in the Netherlands. For all the years of anticipation, as built, it is somewhat stillborn. It looks like a scaled-up model rather than the manifestation of a model idea.

Critics are quick to note its deficiencies as a building. *"In sketches and photos of the model the design remained abstract. And now there it is, like a mirage … , like a scene from a fairytale, because the conceptual radicalism also turned the design into a caricature, a caprice, an object from a world where other rules apply …"* [2] It raises the question of whether the idea, the architecture, did not peak with its model representation. The 28-year gap between the Wall House's conception and construction opens up several uncertainties about the very status of the model as the *representation* of a built work. [3]

The model is conventionally treated in architecture as an issue of representation, either as the anticipation of a thing to come or the documentation of a built project. It can also be, secondarily, a moment of the process where it doesn't have to show the concept as completed, it can be a work in progress. Many philosophical theories of representation have a hard time explaining architectural drawings and models, because the thing represented does not have to exist prior to its representation. This gives rise to a philosophical egg-or-hen dilemma: is the model a representation of the building to be constructed later, or is the building merely the over-scaled representation of the model, as seems to be the case with Hejduk's Wall House?

To solve this dilemma, it may be enough to repeat that the primary task of sketch or process models is introspective rather than representational in the sense that the process model may not even try to look like anything. This raises the question: how do you think about something that is sufficiently materialisable to be a model, but not sufficiently materialisable to become a building? Hejduk's original model for the Wall House is not a miniaturisation of a larger, real building. The model indicates its own exteriority and seems to lack nothing. The commonplace idea of reference is implicated as a presumed ontological lack. A word is needed because the object referred to is unavailable. Similarly, an architectural model is needed because the object it represents, the building, is not yet there. What this idea neglects to consider is the materiality of the sign. Drawings, models and other representations not only point to the referent, but they also have to accept their own conditions of material existence. These conditions entail an excess; any sign or any model always says something more and something else than what might be identified with the referent.

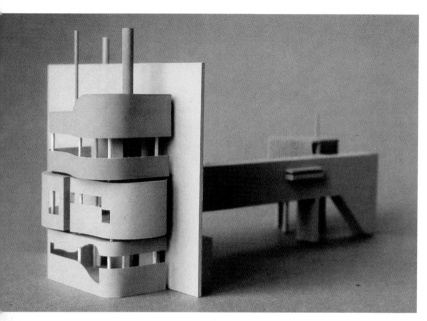

Left
John Hejduk, The Bye or
Wall House model from the
Netherlands Architecture
Institute collection, 1973.
Featured in *Idea as Model*,
Hejduk's model is conceptu-
ally anchored to its scale
and its status as a model.
A good example of a model
that lacks nothing, it exceeds
its functionality as a sign for
a building; the posthumous
building is a sign of the model

On the other hand, with the case of most other models, this notion can be turned around. If a standard model is to be realised as a real building, you imagine it to say *I lack something that must be manifested as built*. A model that doesn't seem to lack something isn't a model in the representational sense. For the normal model to function as part of a chain of process, it can be thought of as lacking. Once it is autonomous, as with Hejduk's Wall House, it isn't a standard architectural model. There is usually a compromise when the model faces the resistance of materiality, drawing a distinction between models as a normal process of architecture and models where 'objecthood' has arrived too soon. The Wall House is a clear example where models can exceed their representational function.

Problems of Model Representation

The problems of model representation lie both in the slipperiness of the model's functionality and in the expectations of representation itself. Christian Hubert brings up this point in *Idea as Model* right away:

> But the truth of the model does not lie in its referential nature since, as simulacrum, the model denies the possibilities of its own autonomous objecthood and establishes the building as the ultimate referent, as a reality beyond representation. It is perhaps the articulation of representation itself which seeks a resuscitation of a 'reality' beyond the limits of the sign
>
> Because some models represent either something that will be built or something that has been built, others are in the position to assert the same privilege of representation and receive similar attention with no real aim of being built. Models intentionally built outside the circuit of manifestation tend toward extreme

Architecture and the Miniature

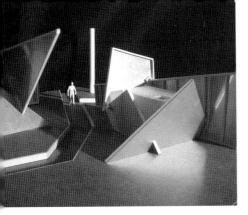

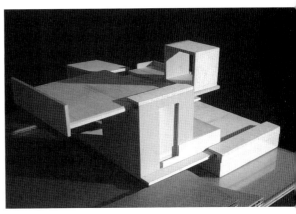

representations having no place outside themselves and are typically utopian or dystopian; both are a stake in ideality, one by example, the other by contrast. They have nothing else to prove, being freed from certain constraints, and can therefore be the site of purely critical work. In Charles Pierce's terms, the model is an iconic sign that refers to its referent by resemblance, sharing some of its characteristics. The scalar relation, because of its mathematical regularity, does not appear as an arbitrary convention but as a necessary rule. The model is small but proportional.[4]

Then there is the case of models made with no real expectation of being built in the first place. As models are held to be a general type of representation, Wall House-type models trade on the representiveness of the others; in their very 'modelness' they are read as objects that still represent a building at full-scale. Models built in school tend to exist at such a level of representation, a level that does not hold to sign/referent logic. Mies van der Rohe's Glass Tower project of 1922 was not necessarily meant to signify or refer to anything outside itself. Even though the project looks like a model it makes no claims beyond the representation of an idea. The project looks like a model of a building to be built … knowing full well it never will be. Such an object denies the model's power of mimesis in exchange for something more open-ended. As these models are not really made to represent that which will be built, they are free to represent other intentions.

Another more basic problem is raised concerning legibility and the model's capacity to represent in the first place. Theorists tend to trip over the model as it frustrates a narrative of representation which culminates not in the model but in perspectival representation. One of the benefits of the model generally held is that it is a more readily understandable form of architectural information than drawings including perspective renderings. But there are those

Opposite

Sir Christopher Wren, Great
Model for St Paul's Cathedral,
London, UK, 1674. Still
housed in the Dean's library
on the triforium level near the
south-west tower, the Great
Model eclipses the design as

built in many respects. This is
largely the fault of the model,
ironically, which opened up
debate (as most models do)
and allowed the Royal Commission to require so many
changes

who deny the intelligibility of the model and see no difference between a three-dimensional model and a set of two-dimensional technical drawings. Christian Norberg-Schulz argues in *Intentions in Architecture*: *"As a concretisation the totality is only present in the finished work, but it can be represented in different ways. Such representations are never satisfactory, as most people lack the ability to 'read' drawings and models."* [5] Relating the problems of describing one of the two identical museums in Vienna's Maria-Theresien-Platz, Gombrich doubts all forms of architectural representation:

> *It has also been asked how we can ever know whether a picture or a map represents a particular building. To this the answer is simple. We cannot. ... Books on the history of our buildings provide yet another variant – a wooden model was made of the whole complex of buildings which incorporated real features but was intended to demonstrate certain possibilities of extension and modification. Only those who have independent evidence can tell what kind of information we are intended to receive from this type of object.* [6]

Rudolf Arnheim has no such worries regarding the clarity of the scale model. He outlines the usefulness of the model for designers and 'the average person':

> *Such models, being easily comprehended in the visual field, are much more surveyable than the executed structures. ... It has been shown not only that spatial relations, such as comparisons of size, can be 'read off' from three-dimensional thought models but that the average person is also quite capable of rotating such models either in the frontal plane or in depth if a task requires it.* [7]

Certainly models can be misread and 'independent evidence' (knowledge of the site, orientation, scale indication and so on) does help to clarify. But if the model is deemed to be as professionally encoded as drawings, why then are presentation models, for example, made in the first place? It may be that the model is not a universal object in terms of legibility, it may instead be deeply culturally determined, but that cultural filter is not a professional one. Exposure to miniature representation starts from infancy through toy play and continues, as Lévi-Strauss asserts, as the defining character of works of art. If one allows that models themselves can be legible, then we might turn to the issue of representations of models themselves and, in turn, check their legibility.

Part 1 : Projective Models

It would be a mistake to point to a 'final model' or presentation model as the culmination of previous process models, as if all process models could be folded into an ultimate object. But a final model should aim to represent a project or architectural idea holistically. While process models may adhere to an internal language of the designer – formal shorthand, quick gestures, spatial spot-checks – a final model entails an intention to communicate more broadly. It is truly an object in the world. Final models are rarely the designer's favourite models; compromises are inevitably made in the interest of legibility. Unlike sketch models, final models aggregate intention, reveal a totality.

Sir Christopher Wren's Great Model for St Paul's was offered as a final model *par excellence*, but in its totality the model undid itself. From 1673 to 1674 craftsmen under Richard and William Cleer fashioned the magnificent model of Wren's design at the unusual scale of one inch to one and a half feet. Wren was confident this expensive and painstaking model would impress: *"a good and careful large model* [built for] *the encouragement and satisfaction of the benefactors who comprehend not designs and drafts on paper."* The large model allowed the king and the royal commissioners to put their heads inside and 'walk' through the nave. Unfortunately for Wren, however, the Great Model was all too comprehensible and this opened it to detailed criticism. The changes required of it meant that, for Wren, the model would have to suffice as a statement of his intentions. The cathedral as built was a cruel compromise. Indeed this is one of the great dangers of the finished model, that it weakens the prerogative of the author in favour of its reception:

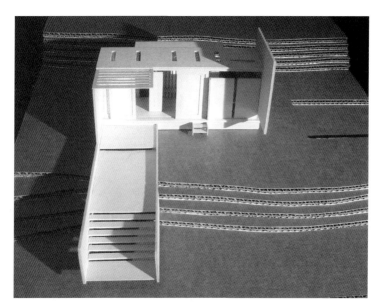

Left
First-year project for a riverside pavilion, 2004. Craft,
scale, proportion and composition are all grappled with
over the course of a modelling assignment. This model
by Brittany Eaker

One can glimpse even in the eighteen-foot Great Model, which is as far as he got with this idea (and after all far enough that some enthusiasts consider that miniature one of the best buildings of its century) how much more cosmic the dome he eventually built would seem if it rose above a symmetrical base like this. The sweeping concavity of the walls mysteriously answers the convexity of the dome, obverse and reverse of a single idea, the most compelling one in the classical repertoire.[8]

Final models are often hastened by deadlines. The project has not truly reached a conclusion, but is forcibly ended according to a schedule. Academic deadlines, reviews, partly mirror such deadlines in the workplace. Outside that, there is an interest in pacing project and ideas in such a way that finality must be forced in order to start anew. Final models are marked by a material change from process models; often to the project's detriment. Final models are wrought in some more lasting material: wood, metal, glass, resin and so on. They require an inordinate amount of time to construct and sizeable investment in material.

The final model stands in for the outcome of only one path of the project idea and hints that any strand of the process might have made something even better. Yet this does not stop its author from presenting it as if it were the finale of the project, the authoritative sign of the idea, only to become frustrated when it cannot fully operate in this way. Final models are about critical anti-climax, pointing to mistakes made in process, in time management, in the idea itself. Given that, what then is the usefulness of such an object?

The last, for lack of which the set at large remains meaningless, is a symbolic summation thereof: it is thereby imbued with a strange quality, the very quintessence, so to speak, of the entire preceding cavalcade of qualities. Certainly, as an object, it is perceived as unique, given its absolute position at the end of the series, which ensures its illusory air of embodying special finality.[9]

Architecture and the Miniature

The final model offers a point of reference within the design process, a place of fixity. Without a deadline, nothing will be resolved. The final model is the horizon of the creative sprint, it guarantees process by eventually stopping it. It allows for critical reflection and puts the idea up for debate, in the social arena. Many students, after documenting their work in portfolios, burn their models at the end of term in celebratory bonfires as a ritual potlatch to unburden themselves of these demanding objects.

The final model, both in school and in the profession, is a place to represent, store and condense ideas. It also serves to prove the dexterity, craft and manual skill of the designer as if it were a building built *in utero*: *"the craft of building models may be seen as the displacement and condensation of the craft of building, an attempt to recover the aura of the work by fetishising the facticity of surrogate objects."*[10] The final model presented at the end of semester to a select jury and peers stands in as the definitive statement of the project. Educators, noting that within the profession projects are handled by teams and not individuals, find fault with the final model's identification with a single author; a holdover from the École des Beaux-Arts and still the prevailing system of studio instruction. Final models in the workplace, by contrast, are rarely touched by the project architect, increasingly they are not even built by the designer's office, but subcontracted to professional model makers. The expectations of the final model are by now so high and its cost so great, that its manufacture cannot be trusted to architects.

Competition Models

A competition model carries the weight of a final model but with even more at stake in terms of critical response. A competition model is intended to win. From the early Renaissance, models are depicted as the chief means of entering architectural competitions and that function continues unabated even as digital displays take over elsewhere. Part of this tradition rests with the make-up of lay competition panels. There is also an element of playing to the judges, presenting an object as a sign of investment in a proposal, a statement of confidence. Competitions depend on the notion that architecture models are universally intelligible.

Two requirements of competitions run at cross purposes. One is to produce a new, daring design capable of satisfying the critics, swaying public opinion and gaining financial backing. The other outlines in minute detail all the spatial requirements and proximities of the proposed building; many of these are outdated even before the building is built.

Competition models are not purely representational. They are also rhetorical devices for the narration of a project. Competition models are not intended to give only a perceptual impression of what buildings might look like when built. Rather, they are primarily intended to persuade the jurors to make a certain decision. You cannot distinguish the model from the presentation in this case. This folds back into the presentation as part of the process of design, at a late stage the project gets tipped towards its 'signature'. For an architect like Richard Meier, the competition model is so bound to his signature that others can readily appropriate his model mode and win competitions pretending to be Meier via presentation. President Mitterrand supposedly selected Carlos Ott's competition entry for the Bastille library project in the hope of getting an authentic Meier.

Competitions can encourage designers with no particular design investment in model making as part of their process, such as Hadid, to fabricate them anyway. There is something bombastic in the presentation of competition models, something theatrical about their unveiling. Competitions are a bet, speculation. Competitions keep architects healthy by periodically offering them the option to conceptualise, idealise and run in the circles they aspire to. They merit an *esprit de corps* within studio in a way nothing else will. Ultimately, a competition entry is a ritual sacrifice of time, energy and expense, like a final model built in school. Importantly, competitions hardly ever require the models themselves, particularly in a first round, so the model arrives to the competition panel as a photograph.

Photographs collapse the three-dimensional model back into pictorial and perspectival space, back to the two dimensions from which it strives to emancipate itself. Perhaps the object-ness of a model, its three-dimensional claims, lies partly outside vision. They are, after all, tactile, haptic and objects in the round. A photograph may capture a single view of a model, but it can refer to more. Problematic as the logistics of the model's representation may be, there is an intuitive sense that there is no problem using a photograph to signal a model, to trigger a three-dimensional understanding of that object versus framing one's reception in such a way as to appreciate the model's representation as an image. Both registers co-exist:

> The 'jealousy' of the model is perhaps most explicit in photographs of models which are virtually indistinguishable from photographs of buildings. The intervention of another form of seemingly motivated representation – namely photography – reinforces the claim of verisimilitude.[11]

To return to the question of the sequence of the sign and referent, in the case where a model prefigures a building, a case could be made for a delayed sign/referent relationship, where the sign comes first. Or, to turn it around, *the model could be the referent and the building merely the sign*. No one accords the model this, but that would tie in more easily with the logic of the sign. In that case – whether the model is represented by a building or painting or photograph – there is no problem so long as the model can be granted the status of referent as it is originary and very often pointed to by architects as the prime bearer of the 'architecture'. Perhaps it would be more useful not to think of models as representation all the time, but in certain instances, consider other representations of the model, acknowledging that the model can function both as referent *and* sign.

Final and competition models must on some level tease the client or critic, putting the project nearly over the top of representation, making the client or critic think partly that the project is already there but for their tacit approval. While at the same time, these models must also hold back from complete autonomy, or else, why should they require building? Things like the Wall House so well worked out to scale are like aberrations when built. As a scale model its characteristics are assumed, so it is a shock to read these qualities when it is rebuilt up-close, habitable and in real time:

> This project embodies an anti-architectural concept which would inevitably lose some of its force if we tried to turn it into architecture, for the purest and most severe concepts cannot enter reality without a loss. When architecture is thinking itself out of existence we would do it no favor by offering it the chance to build its cancellation on a certain street in a particular suburb. … So if one was built – and

Above

Zaha Hadid Architects, Cardiff Bay Opera House, Cardiff, Wales, 1994. One of two final or presentation models for the competition (won but not built). Unlike the sketch models of the auditorium *(see page 41)*, this model introduces colour and texture. Scale is denoted by figures and boats in the bay – context is stressed with the inclusion of the surrounding building and landscape features. The figuration of the auditorium in the courtyard and the wrapping bar of the rest of the complex is clearly established, this frame forming an 'authored' site for the auditorium

maybe this would be a way of taking the thinking more seriously – it would be the model of an idea, and not a house.[12]

Where projects are rendered as pure representation and occupy no real space, these same things as models (and thought models and models as ideas) take up a disproportionate amount of conceptual territory.

The actual Wall House built in Groningen wrenches the Wall House from the model mindset. Eisenman casts the model as a self-reflexive sign with *Idea as Model*, arguing against David Shapiro's assertion: *"A model would seem to be the least reflexive, the most representational of objects".*[13] He explains that the 'Idea as Model' show was organised to test the architectural model as a representation of ideas as opposed to buildings. But a further iteration must prevail: that the model itself can sometimes be a referent – not merely the representation of an idea, but the source of ideas and other representations, the very site where conceptualisation takes place.

Zaha Hadid   Zaha Hadid Architects
Placa de las Artes, Barcelona, Spain   2001

Peter Eisenman   Eisenman Architects
Regional Music Conservatory and
Contemporary Arts Centre, Tours, France   1993-4

The start of most projects involves research of the site environs and the building of a site model in advance of design work. Preparation of topography, surrounding streets and buildings prepares the idea for the project itself. Typically the site model is rendered monochromatically and with less detail than the model of the proposed building. The site model allows a delay in the preparation of a new design by offering a rehearsal of strong existing features. But a site model is, of course, itself designed. Sometimes site models can be as visually arresting or even more interesting than the model building intended for it. The site model allows the project itself to simmer in its own creative juices, as it were, and communicate much more than the model of the building alone ever could.

For Zaha Hadid, the site model *is* the project – it sponsors the intended building, landforms shift and tear to receive the programme.[1] Ramps and canted floors seem to extend the ground plane into the buildings. As modelling moves from paper to more finalised materials (resin, Plexiglas and so on), a whole series of refinements and details are introduced, but the gesture of the paper models remains intact. There is in Hadid's drawings and model work a sense of surface tension generated by this complete integration of site and building through the vehicle of the model.

When the site is a theoretical condition for a project, its modelling is crucial. A large body of Peter Eisenman's work, dating back to the 'Idea as Model' show, is site models acted upon to reveal a scheme through scale manipulations and palimpsest decodings of site memory traces. Eisenman's design for the Tours Arts Centre is all about its site model. Two existing nineteenth-century buildings sponsor a third new building between them by morphing together in stages. This is done very literally with the model. Each existing building's contours and facade is mapped and progressively distorted to match the other, this distillation is captured in the proposed centre, it is equally both the other buildings in form, a fractured and characteristically complex structure entirely sponsored by the transformation of site.

Importantly, Eisenman's signature abstraction of form is postulated early on in the standard simplification of the site model. The existing buildings are rendered to the level of detail expected in a site model and these in turn allow the architect's design to appear as a direct result of a site model process. Authorship of the form of the new arts

Right
Research models, like this one of Zaha Hadid's Plaça de las Artes, isolate one aspect: here the interrelations of the internal volumes

Left
Peter Eisenman's substantial project for Tours is completely wedded to its site, which is modelled in such a way as to underscore the proposed building's contextual fit despite the unusual form it takes. It also happens to look like an educational model of some historic site acted upon strategically

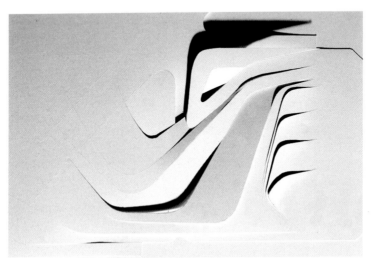

Left
One of several shallow relief models made to study the site of the Plaça de las Artes project and suggest a design for the complex

Right
Layers of paper are used to achieve this relief. Reveals and shadows are as important to the composition as the surfaces themselves

Above
A more finalised model, almost appearing digital in perspective, showing site and complex in a limited colour palette

centre is refused by notionally giving the project over to its site, but this only hides the critical decisions taken with the site model in the first place. Such a project reveals that a site model is never really about accurate documentation of a building's situation, but documentation of another kind, namely, the architect's own filler of the world. You can see in the academic studio design process models as process, final models as representation and site models as documentation; all of which come together as a critical series.

Whereas Eisenman's music conservatory uses existing buildings to extrapolate a new one, Hadid typically harnesses the landscape in an effort to make her proposed building appear rooted to the site (even when that site might be urban, as with the Rosenthal Center). Both are different approaches to the idea of syntax, both try via the site model to insist on their emergent existence and appropriateness to the design problem. Their legibility as proposals is bound to their model manners, their broad sense of 'scape' and how that can be represented artificially in models.

assemblageSTUDIO

Eric Strain, José Gámez, Doug Schneider and Adrian Jones

Mesquite Fine Arts Center, Mesquite, Nevada, USA   2002

The final model for the Mesquite Fine Arts Center aims at verisimilitude. The inclusion of real lighting to show its night-time appearance is only the start. Texture is important to the design, so the materiality of the model mimics full-scale materials: copper, glass, corrugated paper is painted to suggest the patina of weathered roof panels. The silo element is even varnished a coppery green. Cork suggests the desert floor of the site. Dried flowers stand in for wispy desert vegetation. All this exceeds Alberti's model limitations, but this is precisely what many clients expect, particularly for civic commissions, which need to gain public approval and funding.

However, there is more to this model's realism than mere appearance. The architects, wishing to use local materials, suggested that the walls of the centre's gallery be constructed of rammed earth. To prove the feasibility of this procedure and the aesthetic merit of the thick striated walls they recommended, the final model's gallery walls were built as miniatures in rammed earth, complete with scale formwork, formed layer upon layer. What is

more, this construction process was documented and presented as part of the design package. Such a move has historic precedent going back, for example, to Filippo Brunelleschi's models for the dome of the Duomo in Florence where tiny scale bricks were baked and used to illustrate in model the unusual herringbone coursing proposed for the real thing.

With the rammed earth model, you begin to appreciate an architect's typical frustration in designing but not actually constructing buildings. A model can serve to mitigate or bridge this gap in manifestation. Christian Hubert in *Idea as Model* described the creative tension associated with attempts to model not only for formal appearance but for something closer to construction itself: *'the craft of building models may be seen as the displacement and condensation of the craft of building, an attempt to recover the aura of the work by fetishising the facticity of surrogate objects'.*[1]

You might argue that this displacement is essential to the design process and, further, that without the aid of the surrogate/model, formal and structural innovations might not be tried in the field. It may be perfectly healthy for architects or, for that matter, students of architecture, to approach certain models as tiny construction sites where materiality and tectonics get fuller attention. From

the rammed earth model's documentation, you can see the architects literally getting their hands dirty trying to prove the efficacy of their proposal. Following the logic that if it can be built convincingly to scale (which it can), the exercise helped educate everyone involved about an alternative construction technique.

As with Wren's Great Model for St Paul's Cathedral, the Mesquite Fine Arts Center model opened the door to much scrutiny as there was little ambiguity provided to delay judgment. At the same time, the inclusion of so much detail made a relatively small complex seem rich and varied and worthy of its ambitious programme: to celebrate local artisans and history, providing a cultural focus to a quiet resort town just a few miles from glitzy Las Vegas. Although winning the commission, despite all their work with the model the rammed earth walls were not approved by the client.

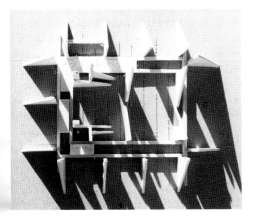

Above
The emphasis models put on
a roofscape (the so-called fifth
elevation) is met with attention
to materiality, even patina, on
certain elements, but the model
does not pretend to be a real
building as photographed

Right
Continuing the theme of the
model as a rehearsal for the
actual construction, the pour
is done in stages to achieve
the striated appearance of
rammed earth

Left
Results of a successful pour:
note the fairly accurate scale
of the bracing members and
the realistic detritus and construction waste

Daniel Libeskind

World Trade Center, New York, New York, USA   2003
The Jewish Museum, Berlin, Germany   1999

Most of the offices submitting proposals for the site of the World Trade Center chose computer renderings as the dominant images to communicate their projects. Daniel Libeskind's, by contrast, focused on a photograph of a model early on. After the shortlist was drawn up, all the remaining contenders did supply scale models and these were exhibited in the Winter Garden near the site to unexpectedly large crowds. More than 100,000 'unique visitors' [1] viewed these miniature cityscapes, far more than those visiting MoMA during the same time. Newspapers commented that the models turned out to be the defining exhibition of the year.

As the six finalists' projects were narrowed to two, THINK and Libeskind's, it was clear that the jury had reacted to the public comments on the model exhibition. Unlike many of the other schemes included, Libeskind had taken on the popular request for an even taller structure than the Twin Towers and included in model form a thin tower-spire. He even made the height of his spire 1776 feet, the year of American Independence. He won for many reasons, but certainly one comes down to his initial real model and its scalar pact with the sublime.

Another reason for Libeskind's success had to do with his forceful narrative. He outlined how inspiration for his tower design was taken not from the ruined Twin Towers nor any other skyscraper,

but from the Statue of Liberty; an odd precedent for a building, but one that makes sense in terms of narrative. [2] A colossus in the classical sense, Liberty is a scaled-up figure. The model tower's actual height of so many inches is conceptually superimposed by its intended height, 1776 feet, the same number carved in Roman numerals on the front of Liberty's book. With this emphasis, Libeskind's scale model was always the biggest in the room conceptually. It was, of course, more or less the same size as the other submissions, but those models emphasised form rather than scale.

Libeskind's thin spire completes the task of tallness or tallest-ness and seems even taller than the other submissions owing to its slimness and proximity to the middling heights he has created to anchor it. He won his biggest commission (we know now this victory was temporary) with the tallest building in part by never forgetting the smallness of the medium architects communicate through. Press releases concentrate on an image Libeskind offered in his shortlist presentation, a photograph of the Statue of Liberty in the foreground with his project peeking over the Manhattan skyline across the water in the background.

Libeskind's models have consistently been model models, or models crafted as much for their own sake as for the buildings they are meant to

In this aerial view of the Jewish Museum in Berlin, the model and the selected elements of the site start to look like a Constructivist painting; quite a different representational strategy when compared with the World Trade Center project *(see overleaf)*. The composition rests on a field of text made up of the names of Holocaust victims

represent.[3] These are models scaled to themselves, their own right size – models fully part
of the showmanship of architecture. The winning
model for his first public commission, the Jewish
Museum in Berlin, is featured on a base wrapped in
what appears to be newsprint (actually the names
of Holocaust victims) as a thing in itself, though the
text would have no direct correlation in the finished
building.

His Imperial War Museum of the North in
Manchester was inspired by another scale-specific
material device. In a bravado move in front of the
client jury, Libeskind smashed a hollow clay sphere
and arranged the resultant pieces into a little clump
of a model and maintained this design of happenstance all the way through his final plans. His
narrative in this case, *"a globe ripped to pieces
by war"*,[4] fulfils a similar function to the Statue of
Liberty simile; it suggests vast scale – the Earth
– while presenting the small. The characteristic
shapes and sections of the sphere proved to hold
interest even wildly scaled up. In this instance, the
architect used size/scale discrepancies to generate
form. One notices this shard sensibility in the mid-
rise towers in his World Trade Center scheme. Yet
these are obviously not spheroid, but prismatic, as
if the architect smashed models of conventional
skyscrapers.

Skidmore, Owings and Merrill

Nanjing Greenland Financial Center, Nanjing, China 2007

Models for very large buildings present special challenges. In an effort to economise the size of the model for, say, a skyscraper, the surrounding buildings included in the site model tend to dwindle to nothing visually. Craft issues arise when trying to manufacture a convincing analogue model at a very small scale. SOM's response is not to let the scale get so small as to render the model a souvenir, but to keep it at a size where its site can be clearly rendered (with vegetation and cars no less). This also permits the proposed building to reveal more formally.

There is a noticeable consistency with SOM models in terms of the limitations of their palette, where water is blue and grass is green but all the architecture is white or grey. The level of craft is undeniably high; these models are well-funded pieces of corporate public relations as well as architectural representations. They represent large commissions and often necessitate transport overseas, which requires more than usual care to be taken with the model's strength and packaging.

Other consistencies are found with the firm's model photography, particularly with skyscrapers. To showcase a project's silhouette, dark 'skies' are preferred to heighten the contrast. Care is taken with the cropping of the site. Just enough of the surrounding cityscape is revealed to vouchsafe the proposed building's relative enormity. There is honesty about the model's artificiality, rarely does SOM collage model shots with site photography or digital effects (clouds, lens flares, theatrical lighting). Rather than play up the illusion of height and take the definitive photograph looking up at the sky-scraper, most are shot from the vantage point of a passing bird looking down on the tower. This mirrors the standard way we view models from above and reinforces our sense of mastery over a colossal thing. This trick foreshortens the object in favour of elevating the viewer to the edge of vertigo. With the images of the model for Nanjing Greenland Financial Center, these trademark qualities can all be read.

From the hovering viewpoint of one photo-graph, the antennae spire seems nearly the length of the tower itself; as if to say, these buildings are so tall that we do not need to valorise but visually minimise their height. Another photograph assumes a height halfway up the tower from a couple of city blocks away. Ecological and cultural aspects of the project are given short shrift in these images. The 300-metre-high tower is wrapped by a series of sky gardens *"that wind up the facade like a coiling dragon"*, according to the office, but this is difficult to find in the representation. The design's effort to integrate a piazza, future subway station and gardens at ground level is also repressed. Instead, the needle-like spire takes centre stage. This might be graphically cleaner than the busy streetscape, and less controversial in terms of planning and infrastructural issues likely to erupt at the base of the building.

Above
In orbit of the Financial Center's gleaming spire: the view is unusual but part of the SOM package. Note the selective use of colour and the pitch black background

Below
This is a more normative vantage point, but still not at pedestrian level. A deep blue sky is introduced. The site model does its job by underscoring the relative size of the super-tall skyscraper

Part 2 : Retrospective Models

Joseph Gandy's 1818 ink and watercolour of *Public and Private Buildings Executed by Sir John Soane between 1780–1815* would seem a prime example of the model in a standard projective or anticipatory mode. The painting shows over a hundred projects designed by Soane up until the year of his wife's death. A fictive room capped by Soane's trademark saucer-dome is filled with paintings and models at varying scales, arranged side by side as a model village lit dramatically by a lamp, a model sun. A large Bank of England model holds the midground, while very small models are arranged over the architrave like a city on a Neoclassical cliff. The Bank of England appears again, as model of a model, on a desk in the foreground staffed by a tiny figure, Soane *"dwarfed by his own genius"*. This figure could walk into the model house to the right or pay respects to the model for Mrs Soane's tomb on the far left, emerging from a black veil. Model facades, sectional models as well as complete ones are featured. The effect is so unusual and distinctive that, of all the paintings Gandy did for Soane, only this one was directly attributed to the artist in the Royal Academy catalogues.

But Gandy's image is really about documentation. These models represent projects already built. The rendering is a retrospective. Gandy has turned built works, executed buildings, back into models; in many cases where models did not exist for these in the first place. It was this watercolour that prompted Soane to create a Model Room within his house/museum. Eventually amassing twenty models in plaster of restored Greek and Roman monuments, fourteen models in cork of ruins (Pompeii and so on), Soane would insert over a hundred of his own projects within this mix. *"In Gandy's drawing, as in Soane's Model Room, the monuments are displayed without any relation to their particular time or place. [...] They evoke a visionary and imaginative world where ideal, transhistorical, orders and forms may not only characterise buildings but may incorporate those buildings within other buildings."* [14] The conceit of the Model Room was twofold. Soane included his own work alongside classical monuments, as part of it, as though all of it were documentation and part of the same archaeology. It further reintroduced monuments whole that had been hinted at by full-scale fragments (some real, some casts) throughout the museum.

Soane was an advocate of models at a time when few were. He collected them as Grand Tour souvenirs, commissioned models of his own designs and used models as educational tools for his apprentices when most students of architecture never saw them in their training. Soane, a patron of the first English school of architecture, was convinced of the model's usefulness and urged their inclusion in education. *"Large models, faithful to the originals, not only in form and construction, but likewise to the various colours of the materials, would produce sensations and impressions of the highest kind, far beyond the powers of description and surpassed only by the contemplation of the buildings themselves ..."* [15] For Soane the model was chiefly a mimetic device, capable of bringing the Grand Tour (which he enjoyed on a scholarship prize) to every young draftsman, even those who could not afford the trip. Soane's set of plaster and cork models of ancient buildings are highly crafted and detailed because they mean to document accurately and broadcast 'the power of the original'. Models of his own projects, in turn, try for the same level of accuracy as they mean to equal their precedents.

But there is little evidence to suggest Soane used models in the earlier stages of his own design process. He committed most projects to paper before ordering a model be made. However, Soane's collection of models served as a vault for ideas during every phase of design; he relied on previous models – often quoting both the classical set and his own models – as vehicles for further creativity. By keeping his Model Room as an expanding archive, nothing was wasted, not even failed proposals like his design for the Houses of Parliament:

> *Models free us from literal constraints to make impossible comparisons with ease, Soane's models invite imaginary perambulations in which the eye is overwhelmed by one thing, then another, creating a phantasmagoric experience: the spatial art, which requires travel, has been internalised.* [16]

Soane documented everything. He designed special cabinets for all of his drawings and pivoting wall panels to display watercolour facades and plans. But the models were perpetually on display, under glass, always visible where the drawings were not – these had to be actively accessed, the models merely passively enjoyed. As miniatures, all the models were treated as curiosities.

Ex Post Facto Models

Models can function as an architect's record and reservoir of design. Conserving past projects, failed competitions and models simply built on a whim, an archive provides a set of objects to return to for inspiration in future. Models collected and displayed within studio or in the office offer a self-generated library of forms, a three-dimensional palette that constitutes personal collection of precedents; the chance to quote one's self. The power of the archive partly lies in the guesswork as to what may be important in future, what may come in useful at a later date. There is a compulsion to save as much as possible for any eventuality. When the model collection becomes unwieldy, as in Gehry's office, another form of documentation must be implemented. Every other week models are thrown away but only after they have been photographed and committed to a file on the project.

In recent years there has been a trend in exhibition display to offer superlative architectural models of projects that never existed as buildings or even as models. Such exhibits are not objects representing architectural ideas, but documentation of such. These objects fabricated as historical props insert model materiality to what had hitherto been mere architectural conceptions, pure 'paper architecture'. One of the most far-reaching of these post-facto types is located at the Salt Works of Chaux, Arc-et-Senans, in France. The Salt Works, designed by Claude-Nicolas Ledoux in 1775–6, is a radial town plan of Neoclassical factories, storehouses and housing. Most of Ledoux's designs were never built, but hold a place in architectural history and theory as supreme examples of *l'architecture parlante* on paper, architecture that speaks or reveals its intended use through its form. Since 1995, Ledoux's life works, the few built and the many unbuilt, have been exhibited within the Salt Works. These models are remarkable not as models but as things already known to architects as plans and vignette drawings suddenly rendered in three dimensions as concrete dreams. Through its rigorous documentation, this elaborate collection of all the works of Ledoux more or less built at the same scale, all finished in whitewash, offers an ideal city within an ideal city:

> *From Michelangelo's sketch models, first roughly executed in clay then refined in wood, to the diminutive colossus, some twenty feet long, built by Christopher Wren in the 1660s when designing St Paul's Cathedral, historical models continue to exercise an enormous fascination. Yet often now they are more admired for their craftsmanship and their perfection as complete, hermetic miniature worlds than for any historical information they may vouchsafe.*[17]

Why would a model be made of a built work? This goes back to fundamental questions of representation. If the model's assumed job is to prefigure a built work at a scale, then its role ex post facto seems illogical. Design students in their first year are customarily required to build a scale model of some famous building. Ostensibly this task is organised to teach the basics of model craft, as if the subject of the model were inconsequential. Really, the basics of model building are already known to the student; or anyone who has previously built a model aeroplane. The purpose of the assignment is to initiate the student into architecture through the mimetic act of modelling some building they might admire. Through modelling, say the Villa Savoye, the student vicariously becomes Le Corbusier – and a kind of associative power is transferred in the process of replication. This is also an indoctrination into Modernism, the assumption being that architects must come to love Modernism, an architecture that they can model readily. Any student today would be discouraged from emulating historicist styles not the least because these are fussy to model. Modernism's palette of form is particularly allied to modelling.

Site Models

The start of most projects, especially academic, involves research of the environs and the building of a site model. Preparation of topography, surrounding streets and buildings prepares the idea for the project itself. Typically the site model is rendered monochromatically and with less detail than the model of the proposed building. The busy work of site modelling in school is usually the only group activity of a studio. The site model offers a delay in the preparation of a new design by offering a seeming rehearsal of the strong features on site. But a site model is, of course, itself designed. Sometimes site models can be as interesting as, or even more interesting than, the model building intended for it.

With many site models a hole is left in the fragment of the miniaturised cityscape or landscape awaiting the proposal. This disturbing gap prompts the strategy for the proposed building's design. The site model is a conceptual vehicle not in its form but in its absence. This blind spot of the site model is profound, it doesn't really exist on site, it often assumes demolition of existing structures, so in this way the gap is completely outside the function of documentation. Yet, without this hole, conceptually, the project cannot proceed. The physicality of the site model, its weight, size and scope, offer other advantages and disadvantages to the architect. Whereas a model itself is portable, a site model seldom is. As an object it is typically grounded in a certain location in studio and only moved for special presentations, it has a locality. When a model building design is slotted into it, its reading shifts. Suddenly the model is not

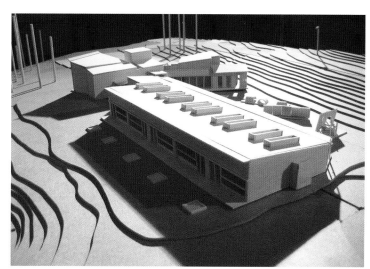

Right
Michael Ward, design for a Kindergarten, The University of North Carolina at Charlotte, 2005. A standard academic final model crafted in basswood and set in an abstracted site of MDF. Monochrome, fastidious and cognisant of the visual emphasis of the roofscape, the model is as much built for its presentation as it is intended for its site, a ravine near the college

Right
First-year projects for a riverside pavilion, 2004. These
projects are the first 'final'
models the students produce.
Most appear unhampered by
preconceptions about what a
final model should look like

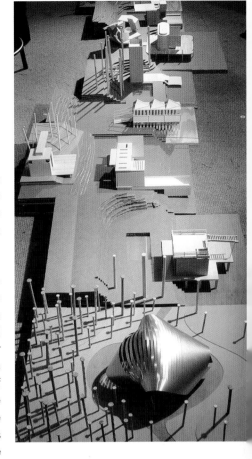

conceived as a totality in itself. Rather, its formal and material assemblage now answers to a wider range of forms in the object of the site model. This can be an advantage or a hindrance. Some models look awful *in situ*, others only come alive in the site model.

The customary repression or awkward-ness in the documentation of landscape elements and people in architects' site models is worth noting. Whereas geometric forms and architectural details can be scaled down, their reading is uncompromised so long as proportions are maintained. The inclusion of trees or figures is always fraught as these elements betray rather than reinforce the model's scale. The fix for this is sometimes had in abstracting trees and people to the point that they mimic the abstraction of the site model itself; this includes making them monochromatic and geometric. In a sense this is already done with the site model where contours in the landscape are rendered as a cascade of topographical steps (directly quoting survey maps) or, more recently, mimicking the geometric mesh options offered by the computer. When this is done in an attempt to make the site sympathetic to the proposed design, its qualities will determine the character of the site model's mode of documentation.

Soane's Model Room involves the siting of each model as an object in the space of a room. When one isolates the model to underline its integrity as an architectural object on a pedestal – what does that say? The wish to have no context is not possible to satisfy ever without a site model; in its absence the studio, the office or the gallery becomes site. This ensemble is the totality of objects for that document, the Model Room. Soane formulates a world where models are placed together from entirely different periods producing a fantastic urbanism that does and does not do what a city does: they're adjacent, but none competes for territory.

Are site models ever purely documentary? A site model can be projective. A model type partly depends on the function it is asked to fulfil. The same model can realise different functions. There is often an internal differentiation within the model so that part is documentary while the model of the project serves other purposes – that mixing serves to persuade people its rhetorical function. The viewer of such a model first can observe the known and then move into the model-as-proposal, that is part of its success: contextualisation. The project does not have to demonstrate a well tempered relation to its environment, it can be an object that reanimates a dormant context. Contextualisation means knitting together the documentary and the projective in a seamless way. The response to a model in its modelled context should be, 'Good Lord, that's real!' as opposed to, 'That's a great proposal'. One falls in love with a project because one has already fallen for the site's representation. The site model need not accept one function.

Laboratory Models

A test model is a documentary model taken a step further. Architectural models of a kind are often used in laboratory testing. They principally relate to aspects of fluid dynamics. Aerodynamic analysis is the most common, but they are also employed in acoustic and construction systems analysis – particularly earthquake testing. Computer simulation now augments such research, but scale models are still built and documented in testing environments and simulated catastrophes. Architectural history bears witness to a number of buildings thought sound at one scale that were compromised at another.

Designing structures to resist failure during earthquakes is done with scale models, usually at a scale of 1:4. These are placed on a shaking-table (a special platform fitted with hydraulic actuators) and measured for deformations or failure in a simulated earthquake, including aftershocks. This research is then compared to computer simulation and analysis of the same. Model bridges and dams are also treated in this manner. Wood, concrete and steel structural systems are tested in model form.

Wind tunnel tests have a range of applications. Measuring for aerodynamic forces, pressure distribution and aero-acoustic levels, scale models are mounted in a wind tunnel and put through a series of simulated atmospheric environments including calibrated wind speeds up to hurricane force. Groups of scale buildings can also be tested for, say, their cumulative effect on a windswept plaza. Proposed train and underground stations designs can be examined in wind tunnel environments complete with model trains: *"The train drag was improved by means of relatively simple modifications of the train nose and roof; shape and positioning of ventilation openings were optimised. The wind climate in and around railway stations and the wind loads on the structural elements were measured in detail ..."* [18] Smoke can assist in the visualisation of air flow, the column of air forced in front of a speeding underground train can be seen drifting through the model station.

The model does not need to be identical to the proposed building – this is not about accurate appearance, but replication of a building's geometry and structure. How do you replicate the forces acting upon it? With the lab model, appearance is no longer the central test, but replication of all the forces (object and environment) comes to the foreground. Since a combination of conditions which a real building might be subjected to cannot be achieved with the test model, the lab does them as a series one by one. The model's scaled down and controlled destruction seems a ritual to guarantee (with the stamp of science) that the real building will stay up.

Peter Wong and Students

The University of North Carolina at Charlotte

Models of various Adolf Loos Villas 2002

Models that document existing structures can be useful analytical tools. Through modelling, say, a challenging building by a favourite architect, architectural lessons might be learnt and applied to one's own work. Such lessons are often more intense than studying a plan or photograph. In many ways accurately modelling a precedent building is more demanding than modelling your own design. Taking measurements from scale drawings and applying them in real space is surprisingly difficult even with the most exhaustive documentation at hand. Stairs and roofs typically pose problems and demand a certain amount of guesswork or triangulation from other elements. The site is another consideration, particularly sloped or other- wise irregular topographies.

Modeling this way can be tedious, but the pay-offs are substantial. Recreating a building to scale, working backwards from customary ways of modelling, rehearses its design in a visceral way. To know the building inside and out, to build it plane by plane, commits it to memory like nothing else can, even visiting the real thing does not offer that whole and simultaneous experience offered by this sort of modelling. Once built, the model can be studied under different light conditions or held at eye level for non-digital fly-throughs.

This series of models assigned by associate professor Peter Wong uses the documentary model as a pedagogical device. To give students access to the spatial complexity of the work of Adolf Loos (1870–1933), a series of model case studies is undertaken. Each model is conceived as two halves that come apart to reveal the building's section and structure. These section models help to illustrate Loos' layering of spaces and interior views achieved by staggering and splitting floor levels. The frequent change of ceiling heights, the push and pull of terraces popping the building envelope and the use of the staircase as threshold are all well handled by the section model. Concepts like Loos' *Raumplan* (literally, 'room plan', concerned with interlocking room volumes based on functional and symbolic hierarchies), developed through projects like his Steiner House, Villa Müller and others are intrinsically understood through this kind of object lesson.

The site is rendered simply in chipboard, but does show where a villa might transform from a two- or three-storey building on one elevation to sometimes five stories on another. The models themselves are of basswood of varying thickness to denote exterior versus interior walls, most floor slabs show simple framing. Doors and windows are all rendered as voids, putting an emphasis on surface, space and shadow.

Below
A detail view of one of
several sectional models,
made during an assignment
designed to help students
explore the spatial complexity
of Adolf Loos' work

For students, this kind of exercise offers revelations about formal complexity, sequence, axes, proportion, and relationship between facade and internal layout; with Loos the starkest of elevations cloak intense arrangements of interiors. Any preconception of a building as so many evenly spaced floor slabs to be apportioned in plan is overridden with this project. In their own subsequent work, students can avail themselves of working primarily in section, both in model and in drawing. Theoretical arguments pitting the *Raumplan* against Le Corbusier's Free Plan become more concrete after such an exercise and might be more readily applied. As all the models for a given seminar are built to the same scale, the villas can be collected and compared, organised chronologically or by formal characteristics. A biography of the architect is offered in this way, a biography perhaps more useful to the student concerned with targeting specific architectural questions and developing a richer architectural language.

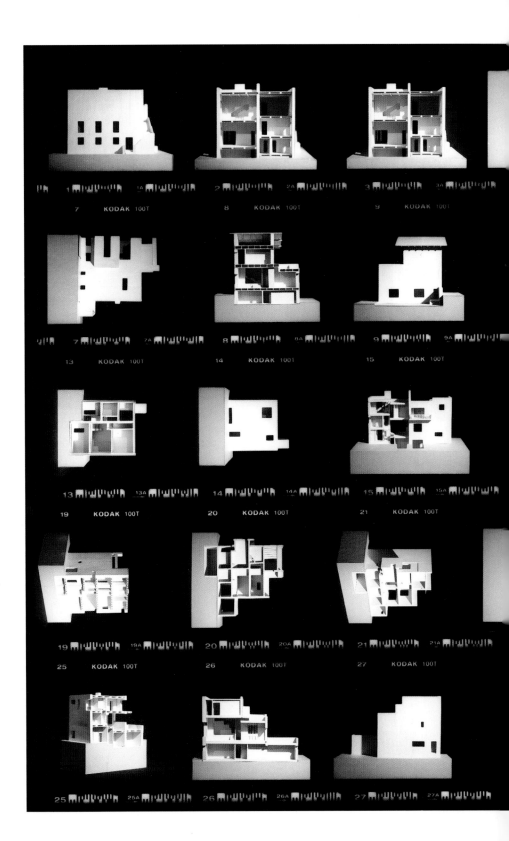

Architecture and the Miniature

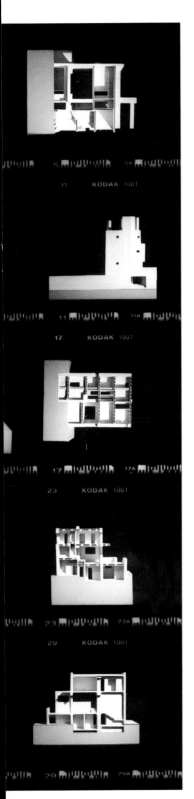

Left

Peter Wong's seminar assignment works on many levels, offering an architectural history lesson, spatial analysis, a test of model craft and a basic understanding of construction. The series is a retrospective of Loos' residential work and identifies the consistent language the architect employed throughout

Below

A close-up view of one of the models, all made to the same scale but to varying levels of detail

Greg Snyder with Bill Bamberger

Mobile Gallery, USA 2002

The Mobile Gallery was a collaborative effort between the photographer Bill Bamberger and architecture professor Greg Snyder. An innovative project, Snyder created a series of equally innovative models for a structure that would house documentation of affordable housing communities (Habitat for Humanity and others) across the country. *"The gallery had to fit in a standard cargo container to be transported from site to site, and so the design evolved from a single unit into a three-piece set of 'rooms' that can connect to one another in a variety of configurations."*[1] Basic models in white matte board were used to explore multiple combinations of the gallery volumes connected by a planar deck. A double-height piece was developed; intended to be set on its side during transport. Once the ensemble was roughed out, another model was built to illustrate its placement on flatbed trucks.

The final 1:8 scale model was finished to an unusually high degree of craft and realism. This, in part, was intended as a convincing fundraising tool. It was also useful in gauging typical layout of photography and lighting. Most importantly, the eighth-scale model was used as a rehearsal in miniature of the real construction of the gallery. This included fabricating accurate miniature versions of off-the-shelf materials including typical 4 x 8 ft corrugated sheet metal panels, sheets of plywood,

wall sections and steel framework. Where certain panels were designed to pivot or slide, they did so in the model. Construction drawings followed from the model and any structural innovations it inspired. Fabricators were shown the model as well as given drawings. The technique streamlined construction as everything conformed to a pattern that conformed to standardised building materials. Doubts about the gallery's feasibility as a display space, its true mobility and its on-site reorganisation were mitigated by careful, if not obsessive, modelling.

Perhaps owing to the tight conceptual fit between model and building, or to limitations on size given the requirement to move the project from place to place, in photographs the model seems larger than the built gallery. Indeed, in photographs the model could well be mistaken for a building. Even with people in a shot of the built gallery, it appears as a large model. This may have been intentional as the Mobile Gallery was designed

Opposite
An arresting vignette that teeters between model and full-scale. Galleries often use models and plan exhibitions with miniatures of the artwork, though the intent here is not solely curatorial

Right
Ghostly models of the mobile gallery components on flat-bed trucks. These were laser etched and cut, the careful lighting used here augmenting the sense that these could be wire-frame digital models

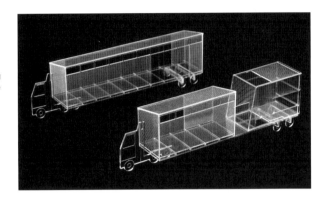

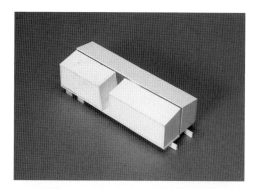

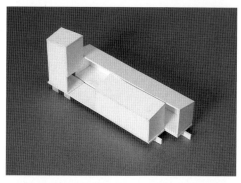

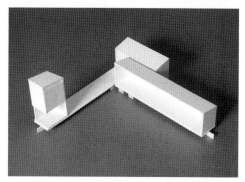

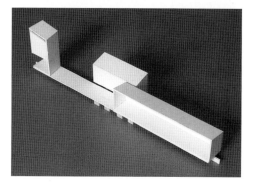

Above

The model's main entrance elevation dramatically lit internally and externally

Right

Four permutations of the proposed gallery elements, some more dense and autonomous (more building-like), while other options stretch and interrelate across distance (more city-like)

Architecture and the Miniature

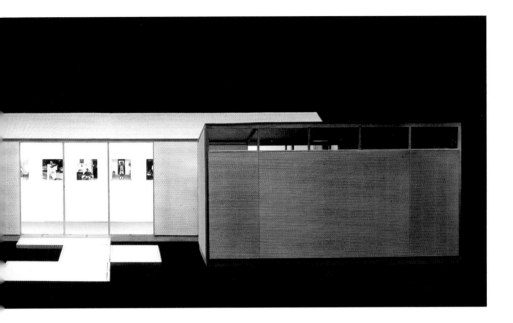

to repress the institutional scale of galleries and museums in order to invite wider public participation. Just as Walt Disney's Main Street is undersize to entice visitors (making one feel slightly bigger in the world), so too does the Mobile Gallery shrink or appear model-like as built. At the same time, this sense of shrinkage is achieved by playing with preconceptions of streetscapes or galleries and their accustomed size.

Although models included a deck or raised terrace space early on, its role was understated largely because it read as building site for a site-less building. As built, the exterior deck became as significant as the gallery interiors, functioning as a connective public space; it hosted workshops, parties and night-time slideshows. This exterior space defined by the gallery became the icebreaker for many unsure about entering the gallery proper straight away. Here the deck becomes the smallest plaza edged by mini-buildings. Part mobile home, part prefabricated unit, the Mobile Gallery also suggested the Barcelona Pavilion and, with its exterior decking in place, Pienza. On tour in San Antonio, local teenagers offered to 'tag' or graffiti the gallery's exterior which Snyder and Bamberger acquiesced to; the model, however, remained pristine.

Below
An end elevation lit as the long elevation above. These photographs float a realistic model in black space – as opposed to placing it in a mock environment, making it all the more striking as an object

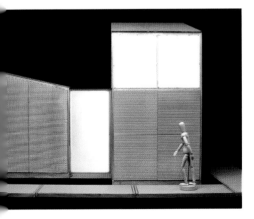

Zaha Hadid   Zaha Hadid Architects

National Centre of Contemporary Arts, Rome, Italy   1997
Rosenthal Contemporary Art Center, Cincinnati, Ohio, USA   1997

A model from the office of Zaha Hadid should be instantly recognisable. Why? You cannot say there is a model 'house style'. They vary widely in terms of level of abstraction and material palette. One quality common to many of them is their luminosity. They simply glow. It might be said Hadid designs for the nightscape. Many of her paintings jumpstart or encapsulate her architecture projects in a black or darkly coloured field. But the attraction is not that these models make reference to sophisticated or dangerous night-time; it is not a metaphorical thrill. Rather, it is the attraction our eyes have to a candle lit after hours. One's attention is held by the light emanating from the object of the model and the contrast that renders, not a fantasy concerning the proposed building's nocturnal appearance. This interest comes partly from novelty. Most models assume daylight conditions and play up the beauty of shadows and reveals. Many of Hadid's models forgo that sort of beauty for another.

Take, for example, the 'day' and 'night' views of Hadid's National Centre of Contemporary Arts in Rome. The model itself is well made and complex, without bowing too much in the direction of veri-similitude. The site is minimally rendered, but enough to show the immediate context and the basis for the width of the 'bars' that make up the compo-sition. There is a nice visual ambiguity between the shadows and the dark translucent envelope wall that wraps each 'bar'. A good model by day ...

By night, every element filters or channels a light source hidden in the base of the site model. Each bar includes translucent and transparent pieces (representing roof trusses, cross beams, internal partitions) that filter light variably. Floor slabs and ramps, being thicker plates of Plexiglas, channel light to their edges. The smoky walls filter less light and frame the space of the galleries. Where many planes overlap, the light dims; the light level works as a diagram showing where the section becomes dense and where it thins out. The only shadows cast are silhouettes of the proposed building seen on the opaque site model. The bend and curve of each bar in plan reads more clearly by day, but the sense that these bars visually and spatially lace and intersect at moments of overlap is best understood looking at the lit model in a dark space. Does the night view obscure the ground plane and diminish one's ability to understand the proposal as a weaving of distinct parts? Yes – the effect of the emanating light on tired eyes renders these parts into a diaphanous whole. Is the project enriched by having access to both visual conditions? Probably.

Other models from Hadid's office only live in darkness, which is to say, they are expressly built as glowing objects and are meant to be viewed as such. The model for another arts complex, the Rosenthal Center for Contemporary Art in Cincin-nati, is not about the nightscape, but how the programme is organised. The entire complex is

Above and **left**
In these views of the National
Centre of Contemporary Arts,
the site is modelled in Perspex
and the bands that comprise
the galleries are rendered as
consistently transparent or
translucent

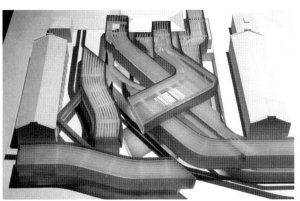

Left
The conventionally lit photograph of the final model *(top)*
shows the material difference
between the proposal and
the site, while the same model
illuminated in darkness *(left)*
purges most of the site and
offers a layered composition
with no sense of intended
scale

Right
With the models for the
Contemporary Art Center in
Cincinnati, even the interiors
get the colour and lighting
treatment. This model shows
how the lobby organises the
circulation and the relationship
to the street

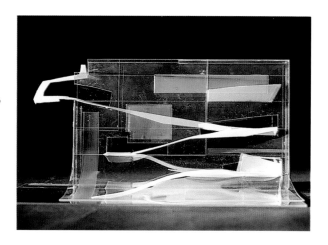

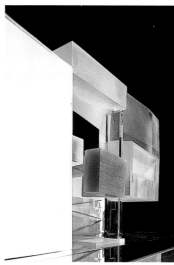

Above
The building's startling edge at
a street intersection rendered
in glowing shades of icy blue

Opposite
Several of the models feature
colour as part of an abstracted
representation of interrelated
spaces or programmatic
elements. The overall profile of
jewel-like prisms corresponds
to later sections and elevations
that abide by a muted palette
of blacks and beiges

represented as a series of moulded resin boxes.
These volumetrically reveal the centre's spaces,
while their different colours signal programmatic
shifts: exhibition, café, theatre, support spaces.
The boxes are also finished differently, juxtaposing
sanded surfaces with matte and glossy. The whole
collection of boxes levitates over the ground floor,
expressing an ambitious design concept to formally
pull the space of the street and pavement into
the cultural zone of the centre to create an 'urban
carpet'. Ramps link the ground floor and street to
the assembly of boxes above, but these are the
only scale indicators offered.

The site is otherwise minimally treated, even
though a good deal of attention is paid to how
the boxes are stacked at the corner of the building
facing a major street intersection, where the boxes
seem impossibly cantilevered. Treating the ground
plane itself as a transparent datum, one can also
see the spaces designed below grade. This model
is not about showing how the building will look –
though it helps explain the geometry of the facade
– but how the design was conceived. Even models
built to examine just the articulation of the lobby,
where the urban carpet lifts and merges with the
back wall of the Rosenthal Center, are built to glow
and colour code. With these it becomes obvious
that the internal lighting of the models is not a
special effect but a mechanism to visualise what
will be largely invisible once built.

David Chipperfield

Literature Museum, Marbach, Germany   2002–5

Addition projects (whether a new wing to a gallery or the expansion of a residence) yoke the site and the proposed building model in interesting ways. Is the existing structure to be modelled as part of the addition proposal, or should it register as part of the site's configuration? This might depend on how integral the addition is or how complex the relationship is between existing and new. If the amalgam is modelled all together, there might be confusion over where existing ends and new begins – the project might also claim too much territory and appear overreaching. With his design for the Literature Museum in Marbach, David Chipperfield renders the addition in a separate colour from the rest and with a pronounced degree of detail, making the new structure special in context.

Sited in a bucolic parkland setting overlooking a river valley, the Literature Museum was recently built to mark the 200th anniversary of Friedrich Schiller's death. The museum is an extension to the existing Schiller Museum and German Literature Archive. Conceived as a series of terraces next to the existing museum's forecourt and overlooking the valley, the model as a whole is positively demure. Galleries meant to display original manuscripts of Kafka and Döblin are, by necessity, only artificially lit. These are linked by descending hallways and public spaces full of natural light and panoramic views.

The model reveals an alternating pattern of dim, wood-lined galleries and bright glassy platforms holding the edge of the building envelope. This is done subtly with hardwood and sanded Perspex set against a deadpan grey model of the site and existing Neoclassical structure. Bushy green model trees seem an aberration, but work as a foil to the straight lines of the addition. Just enough figures are distributed to remind you of the generous scale of the ensemble.

A detail model is also offered, showing a cross-section of one gallery and the adjoining corridor. Structure, colour, modulation of lighting and proportion are neatly expressed in this view. Scale figures are again used, but these seem purposeful, part of a suggested narrative. There is something almost haunting about the way these models are photographed. Part of this sensibility springs from the hardness of the exterior's treatment versus the warmth and variability of the section model's interior; an Adolf Loos aspect. The ethos of the Chipperfield office, a combination of formal restraint alongside care for materiality and texture, is expressed in the museum model as if the model were part and parcel of the firm's output regardless of scale. The same attitude holds for product design and Chipperfield's furniture systems, a consistency difficult to attain.

Below

This detailed section model shows the contrast between the earthy galleries and the connecting corridors, lined with glass and overlooking the valley. Care was taken to model the display cases and shelves, while the inclusion of the figures suggests scale and sequence

Bottom

Simple but effective, the model for the new Museum is set in a basic site model. Topography is rendered as built-up plates, while the existing Schiller Museum and Archive are abstracted as a massing model, without any Neoclassical dressing to take our eyes off the proposed addition

Coop Himmelb(l)au

Wolf D Prix, Helmut Swiczinsky + Partner

BMW Welt, Munich, Germany   2001–6

No architecture office today better employs models as an integral part of the creative process than does Coop Himmelb(l)au of Vienna. The design team, headed by partners Wolf Prix and Helmut Swiczinsky, raids many model types and allocates sizable resources in building analogue and digital models. Their design for BMW Welt (Bavarian Motor Works World), part of a staged competition, was largely achieved through modelling beginning with a series of sketch models carved from blocks of foam and culminating in a shimmering model of polished resin set in a carefully crafted site model showing the new exhibition hall's relationship between the company's headquarters and the Olympic Park in Munich.

A facility meant to celebrate the BMW brand, its history and its future direction, the BMW Welt building includes spaces for tours, meetings, events, car delivery and customer care. Formally, the main exhibition space is sandwiched between an undulating landscape below and a concretised cloudscape above (both of which house smaller elements of the programme). These two meet in an hourglass vortex encircling a spiral ramp intended for cars located at the corner of the complex. The conical geometry of this piece visually ties the new project to the nearby BMW Tower, a high-rise

interpretation of a four-cylinder engine (designed by Karl Schwarzer, another Viennese architect, and built in 1972).

From the start, Prix and Swiczinsky's concept treated the design for the building as a composition of solids rather than planes. Sketch models whittled from sheets of blue foam insulation, fastened with pins and wrapped in plastic film, start to represent the solid-void-solid strata and their formal inter-weaving around the vertical connector. A notion for the ramp lacing through the space is also present early on. A subsequent series of models in white foam focuses on the hovering top element, while others in translucent plastic examine the envelope for the exhibition hall, the void. Basic site conditions are then modelled, giving some context and sense of ground plane.

'Preplanning' models turn to a finer white foam as a material, but these are more exacting and monolithic – the Henry Moore stage of the process. Other models feature a glassy skin, revealing the structure and circulation systems that link the upper and lower strata. Interiors are suggested at this stage and already include model cars and figures. With the addition of the cars, your sense of the intended size of the building shifts. This is a very large complex. Habitual use of pedestrian

Right: above and **below**
An early stage process model in paper investigates the internal topography of the building

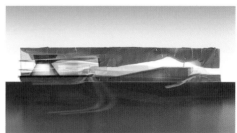

Bottom
This later stage process model of foam and Perspex includes site features. The service spaces are treated as monolithic slabs above and below the exhibition hall

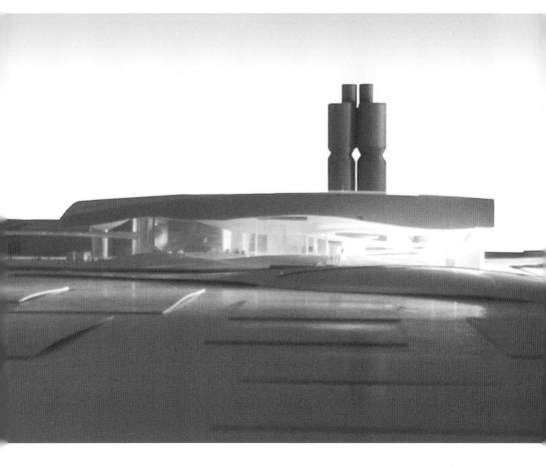

Below
This digital model examines
one section of BMW Welt,
a useful approach given the
complexity of the project

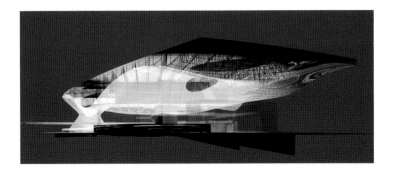

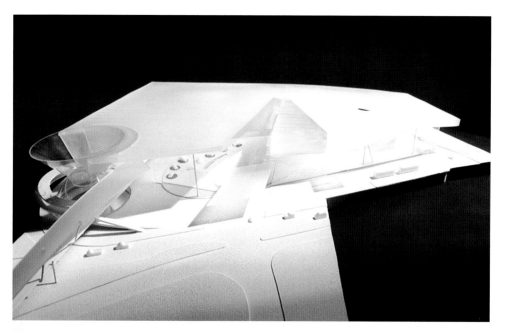

Above
A transparent and translucent
Perspex model introduces
model cars as primary occu-
pants and scale indicators

Opposite
Two views of a later stage
model, internally lit, using
metal mesh over parts of the
elevation. The interiors are
rendered as accurately as the
exterior, and the structure is
carefully indicated. The model
is so fine, it starts to appear
real – if not exceeding any
image of the real thing

ramps in models as scale indicators is undone,
the ramps for BMW Welt are really internal roads.

'Planning' models, as the office refers to them,
include those used to weigh different tectonic and
design options: cladding systems, lighting, structural resolution of ambitious forms. These models
include digital versions that are used to manufacture
prototypes that can be checked in site models and
lit internally in order to gauge the building's appearance at night.

Physical models at this stage incorporate solid
and perforated metal panels snapped to a space
frame that holds the undulating forms. Digital
modelling by now runs in tandem with the analogue,
and the office is able to produce photo-realistic
vignettes of the scheme alongside the models that
still hold to a limited material and colour palette.
Beautiful in their own right, a number of detail
models are built to answer questions specifically
about the design of the vortex which, by now, is
understood as a double cone hugging the spiralling
ramp. Following on from these, a model is made to
study just the body of the roof form and how it
translates to the double cone.

You would think, given the extraordinary
amount of detail worked over in model form thus
far, that any final model would try somehow to
encapsulate all the preceding ones. At the very

least, a final model for a project like this would broadcast the intensity of the others by incorporating many of the details and complexities wrought elsewhere. Instead, Coop Himmelb(l)au produced a model in transparent resin, its surface polished to a golden lustre, a proportionately accurate but highly abstracted object that revisited the thematic clarity and sculptural quality of the early sketch models.[1] Only through an exhaustive modelling procedure does the final model represent not the totality but the essence of the design. It would seem a rather brave step to take in regard to the client and the press covering development of the project, but this glassy model plays on first impressions and crystallises (literally and figuratively) the concept for BMW Welt. With the collection of other models on hand and known to the client, this model can afford not to be definitive, but very clear about the highlights of the scheme: solid/void interplay, the vortex and its presence on the site. Indeed, the resin model seems even more abstracted given the conventional and precise handling of the site on which it rests. It makes BMW Welt appear even more special or alien relative to its context.

Wolf Prix and Helmut Swiczinsky would certainly have problems with the idea that any one of their models is somehow final, relegating all the rest as rehearsals or subordinate to the last. The 'final' model for BMW Welt is not, in truth, final; other versions, mostly digital, will take the project through construction. The resin version is just another model in the series that targets a problem or fulfils a specified function. This 'final' model works primarily as a public relations device, a communication tool intended to summarise the whole project without appearing too fussy or over worked, and one that is meant to be featured in newspapers and magazines. It is a model modelling the design: glitzy, photogenic and memorable.

Left
This digital model collaged with a site photograph starts to link the formal language of the proposal, particularly the vortex piece, to cylindrical forms featured elsewhere on the BMW campus

Below and **bottom**
A different sensibility arrives with this mixed media model. Various ideas for the building envelope are represented and scale figures are introduced

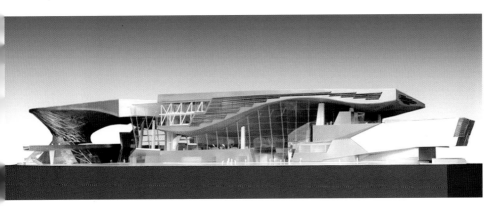

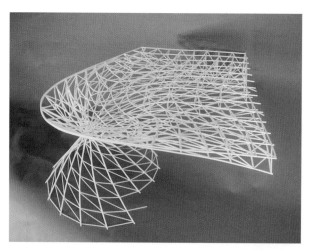

Left: above and **below**
Two views of an analytical
physical model that targets the
structure of the cyclonic ramp
core that anchors one corner
of the building

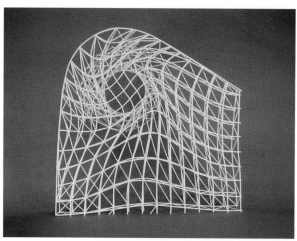

Architecture and the Miniature

Above

The show-stopper model in its site, taking full advantage of the material and formal differences between the proposal and its environs

Opposite

A composite model, combining hand-crafted and rapidly prototyped elements, that studies the approach via the rampway

Model Culture

Models have a cultural context. While models might be widely associated with architecture, things that look like models feature elsewhere in our lives. This by itself may not be of particular interest to the architect, but taking a wider view of what counts as a model (and what a model might unintentionally conjure) may aid in deciding what sort of model to deploy. Clients, committees and competition boards may not be familiar with the professional use of models, but this does not get in their way of reading them accurately. This is largely due to previous exposure to models since childhood. Reasons why the model is more accessible than architectural drawings to the layperson may be found in these supra-architectural types. We are preconditioned to understand miniature objects and therefore models.

This cultural context has an emotive element. There seems to be an agreement among critics that models prompt either desire or nostalgia. John Elsner treats the essence of the small scale in this way: *"In effect, Soane's model world provides a remarkable example of the theme of the miniature and of the miniature as site of desire."*[1] Susan Stewart's sophisticated analysis of scale and things like doll's-houses culminates with the following statement: *"The miniature, linked to nostalgic versions of childhood and history, presents a diminutive, and thereby manipulatable, version of experience, a version which is domesticated and protected from contamination."*[2]

Christian Hubert in *Idea as Model* also speaks of the model in terms of desire and nostalgia in 'The Ruins of Representation'. The model's object status allows for it to be read as an object of desire or, in the psychoanalytical stance, a lost object. Scalar allegiance to things like toys seems to be the most direct tie to nostalgia. Assuming desire and nostalgia are part of the model's reception, we then want to ask the following: What does nostalgia mean for the model? And of desire: how exactly are models desirable? What kinds of models prompt desire and is it possible for the model to pretend to satisfy these? Taking them as given, can we find

out what is really meant by desire and nostalgia for the model through its different cultural manifestations?

Serious Playthings

Toys are miniaturised objects, where the documentary character is of no real interest. Toys lie between the obsessional and the imaginative. The value of a toy rests upon strict representational fidelity as with train sets and doll's-houses. A model misread or not read is a toy. *"To toy with something is to manipulate it, to try it out within sets of contexts none of which is determinate."* [3] If a bona fide architectural model is too costly, model desire/nostalgia can be routed through surrogates. The toy is the most obvious among these. The fact that architectural models themselves are often likened to toys only underscores the obvious links between the two. One critic of Soane writes: *"While a real building can never be fully surveyed or controlled – for it always contains its viewer – the model is the building reduced to a toy. It is architecture the owner can survey."* [4] Another makes the point, *"But his [Soane's] interest in models as serious playthings is something it would be hard to get any practitioner to admit to."* [5] This notion of the model as a 'serious plaything' helps to understand qualities of playfulness attached to sketch models as discussed previously.

Susan Stewart describes the role of the doll's-house as a staging place for adult themes expressed by children and, conversely, its role as time capsule for adults. *"The dollhouse has two dominant motifs: wealth and nostalgia. It presents a myriad of perfect objects that are, as signifiers, often affordable, whereas the signified is not."* [6] Queen Mary's doll's-house was designed by Sir Edwin Lutyens. It took three years and many tradesmen to complete it before being presented at the British Empire Exhibition at Wembley in 1924. This national treasure on

permanent display at Windsor is incorrectly thought to represent a woman's obsession with perfect domesticity. Rather, it was Lutyens' nostalgia and fascination with the miniature that propelled the project. Lutyens had the doll's-house constructed in his own living room. He never tired of drawing details for it even when he was meant to be attending to enormous projects in New Delhi. Lutyens offered several innovations with his doll's-house. It is accessible on all sides – all four facades can be drawn upwards via a system of pulleys. Lutyens even rendered a basement level complete with model motorcars powered on alcohol. The tiny books in the library were specially commissioned and can all be read with a magnifying glass. Real postage stamps double as royal family portraits.

The building block had been a staple of play before Froebel's invention, but did not adhere to any high-minded geometrical programme. Older block sets were, in fact, more overtly architectural containing elements that approximated architectural details. Froebel found these to be too limiting. The most commercially successful twentieth-century building block, LEGO, also came out of a wood block tradition. The Christiansen family of Billund, Denmark began toy manufacture in 1932. After their wooden-toy factory burnt to the ground, they took up plastic injection moulding and created the Automatic Binding Brick. Like Froebel blocks, LEGO pieces are abstracted shapes calibrated in proportion (though not Golden) and from early on LEGO was intended for constructing scale buildings. LEGO advertising is largely based on the appeal of the toy-model and a cycle of building, demolition and rebuilding.

Narrative
Toys are associated with scalar narratives. A great deal of juvenile literature and film is centred on miniaturisation for the obvious reason that children have a special scalar relationship with

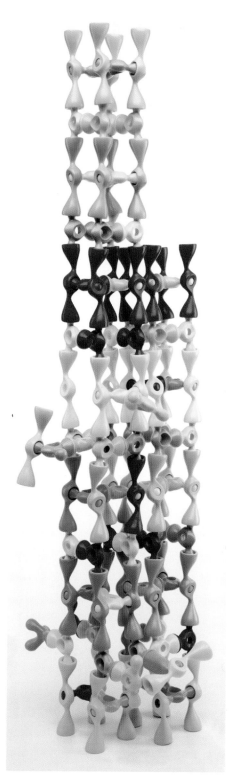

Left

A new breed of plastic block. Daniel Oakley's Öliblock sets eschew the grid and brick typology for a world of curves, concavities and knobs that string together as fantastic chains of colour and varied profile. Zaha Hadid collaborated on the inventive design

Below

Öliblocks as space frames. There is something skeletal or scientific about the structure, hints of DNA models

their environment. From the Brothers Grimm to Disney, narratives for children abound in detailed descriptions of the small. Dwarves, fairies and gnomes are commonplace characters and they all claim scaled-down environments. Toys that come to life or personified animals find shelter in doll's-houses or adapt everyday items like matchboxes as pieces of furniture in some hidden lair. The delight these stories take in minutiae represents a large part of their appeal. Tales rooted in the description of small-scale physical environments are prime candidates for film adaptation. There is an economy in making, say, a stop-animation film based on a scale narrative as the sets are readily built as architectural models. These in turn suggest toys to be marketed with the film. There is no scalar difference between the narrative, film set and merchandise.

Alice in Wonderland plays with scale constantly, as does *The Wizard of Oz*. The Munchkin Village comes from Baum's book, but its fame must be attributed to the film's precious set of half-size thatched cottages populated by the large cast of little people. The journey from Munchkinland to Oz is about arriving back to full-scale. Growing up is again literally translated in *Peter Pan* when the Lost Boys build Wendy a small house (all the boys live in treehouses). The most famous scale story, Swift's *Gulliver's Travels* has had many film treatments focused on the second chapter of the story. Gulliver is intensely involved in the miniature architecture of Lilliput:

> I stepped over the great western gate, and passed very gently, and sideling through the two principal streets, only in my short waistcoat, for fear of damaging the roofs and eaves of the houses with the skirts of my coat. I walked with the utmost circumspection, to avoid treading on any stragglers, who might remain in the streets, although the orders were very strict, that all people should keep in their houses, at their own peril. The garret windows and tops of houses were so crowded with spectators, that I thought in all my travels I had not seen a more populous place. The city is an exact square, each side of the wall being five hundred foot long. The two great streets which run across and divide it into four quarters, are five foot wide. The lanes and alleys which I could not enter, but only viewed them as I passed, are from twelve to eighteen inches. The town is capable of holding 500,000 souls.[7]

When a fire breaks out in the palace, Gulliver saves the day by urinating on the blaze in sight of the Lilliputian queen.[8] For this the hero is banished. Psychoanalyst Sandor Ferenczi describes 'Lilliputian hallucinations', in an elaboration of a point in Sigmund Freud's *Interpretation of Dreams*:

> The sudden appearance of giants or magnified objects is always the residue of a childhood recollection dating from a time when, because we ourselves were so small, all other objects seemed gigantic. An unusual reduction in the size of objects and persons, on the other hand, is to be attributed to the compensatory, wish-fulfilling fantasies of the child who wants to reduce the terrifying objects in his environment to the smallest possible size.[9]

Gulliver's Travels illustrates a desire not to shrink and inhabit a model environment, but to use diminution to become a relative giant. This finds a parallel in the toy's function to defray anxiety and lend a sense of control. All scale narratives, from literature to film and computer games, speak to issues of dominance – overcoming fears, mastering situations.

Cinema forces the question of scale and its relation to the architectural model in part because cinema is by definition completely bound up with scalar relations as a medium tied to projection. Once scale is in place and a logic of relations is established, cinema permits scalar paradoxes. The big size of King Kong is proved by the notional huge size of the Empire State Building through models. The technical friendliness that exists between the camera lens and the model is well known. Despite the advent of digital applications for film, the mode continues to be used, often enhanced by the newer technology. Models take advantage of the monocular camera lens and trick the depth of field:

> *We have all seen scale models of buildings such as the Parthenon, some with little toy manikins dotted around. Now it is obvious that if we bend down to the point where these toy manikins stand, the aspect of the building will appear the same as it would from the corresponding position on the Acropolis. Film producers make use of this fact when they have to represent disasters such as earthquakes. A scale model of a burning house, or a collapsing bridge, can be made to look indistinguishable from the 'real thing' if all standards of comparison are eliminated.*[10]

Science fiction uses scale for effect and narrative. Fritz Lang's *Metropolis* of 1926 is largely successful because it keeps model shots apart from plot scenes with real actors. Lang's pan shots of the model city are used as a foreground to subsequent action, but are

themselves autonomous from the rest of the script. The addition of zooming model aeroplanes and trains routed through the scaled city uses movement successfully to imply duration. George Lucas' 1977 *Star Wars* film uses models in exactly the same way. His nascent Industrial Light and Magic company cobbled together spaceships and battle stations from hobbyists' model car and aeroplane kits. The addition of movement and occasional pyrotechnics offered the illusion of spaceship battles that had hitherto – with serials like 'Buck Rogers' – never convinced. Sublime environments in *Star Wars* were generated from the smallest things. The dreaded Death Star, an armed space station the size of a moon, was a model sphere two feet in diameter. The architecturally vast must be, can only be, represented by models. The charm of iconic architectural images like Le Corbusier's giant hand coaxing out a flat from the Marseilles Block rests with the cultural conditioning *King Kong* and company have provided.

Model Villages and Souvenirs

Model villages are part of the tourist trade and play heavily on the theme of nostalgia. One of the most famous model villages is in the yard of the Old New Inn of Bourton-on-the-Water. Here a Cotswolds town (already a model village of sorts where every building in town is listed) is kept at one-ninth scale. Built in the same local stone as the town itself, receiving over time the same patina as the real, an exact replica of Bourton-on-the-Water is recreated street by street, building by building. Conceived by a previous innkeeper and faithfully constructed by a gang of out-of-work craftsmen, mini-Bourton was dedicated in 1937 on Coronation Day.

Through it runs a metre-wide River Windrush crossed by seven replicas of the town's characteristic stone bridges. These must take, proportionally, much more weight as adults and children cross them, navigating through the model village just as they would the real. Flora in the foreground is clipped just enough that it neatly fuses with the full-scale trees and shrubbery

in the distance. Children stalk the streets like creatures from a science fiction film. The effort here is so maniacal that there is a model of the model village in the model yard of the model inn, and within it, yet another. Under the right circumstances – in afternoon light with few visitors – Bourton-on-the-Water-the-Lesser does what every model village hopes to, it tricks the eye it replaces measure for scale.

A modern model village like Legoland at Windsor is less successful because it is forced to edit a large and complex metropolis. LEGO London is built to a generous scale and set outdoors straddling a tiny Thames lined in dwarf maples. LEGO London is a city of select landmarks only and none in true proportion to the other. The only urban clutter surrounds Trafalgar Square and an abbreviated Whitehall. Big Ben is detached from non-existent Houses of Parliament. LEGO St Paul's is stunning if only for the pains taken to make square-faced blocks approximate classical details.

Souvenirs of local landmarks in the form of miniatures can be found in most major cities. Washington DC hawks bric-a-brac White Houses and Capitols. Paris has its Eiffel Tower. Rome its Colosseum. Moscow churns out paperweights of St Basil's Cathedral. London is distinctive for the scope of its souvenir monuments, none seems to fully capture the city or take over as the superlative symbol. The Tower of London, Buckingham Palace, Tower Bridge, Big Ben, Parliament, Nelson's Column, St Paul's, Westminster Abbey, the Olde Curiosity Shoppe all get more or less equal billing on the shelves of gift shops. Building after building, famous and generic, combine to reinforce a collective image of the city. The Eiffel Tower in some sense stands as a metaphor for Paris, London's monuments are metonyms, an associative chain that extends even to the fictional.

What is the function of the model souvenir? Susan Stewart outlines a case for such things as repositories of a certain type of memory. *"We might say that this capacity of objects*

Opposite
Souvenirs of London. With
no superlative landmark, but
a series of competing ones,
tourist shops brim with model
paperweights, model teapots,
model clocks and the ubiqui-
tous snow globe variety

to serve as traces of authentic experience is, in fact, exemplified by the souvenir. [...] The
souvenir speaks to a context of origin through a language of longing, for it is not an object
arising out of need or use value; it is an object arising out of the necessarily insatiable demands
of nostalgia."[11] Miniatures play to a fantasy of distance. On one level the small representation
of something is merely that same object viewed from far away. Bachelard elaborates:
"Distance, too, creates miniatures at all points on the horizon, and the dreamer, faced with
these spectacles of distant nature, picks out these miniatures as so many nests of solitude in
which he dreams of living."[12] In the case of the souvenir Big Ben, the distance implied by its
small scale signals both a spatial and temporal gap.[13] This feeds into stock notions of tourism,
of collecting souvenirs to remember something/someplace later and far away. Model villages
are souvenirs one cannot purchase or take home. Their aim is to make a locality suddenly
distant and therefore a distant memory even before you leave the place and go home. These
immobile souvenirs trigger nostalgia for a place you haven't left yet.

Art

Depictions of models in works of art are common, particularly with religious subjects. Certain
reliquaries are also very fine models finished in silver, gold and precious stones. But a model
itself can also be a work of art. Scale permits us to read a model as an artwork and vice versa.

> Now, the question arises whether the small-scale model or miniature, which is also
> the 'masterpiece' of the journeyman, may not in fact be the universal type of the
> work of art. All miniatures seem to have intrinsic aesthetic quality – and from what
> should they draw this constant virtue if not from the dimensions themselves? – and
> conversely the vast majority of works of art are small-scale.[14]

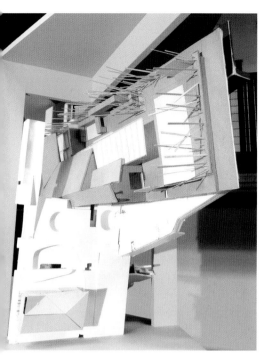

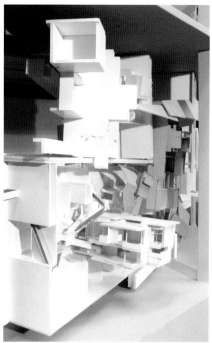

Left and above

Chu+Gooding Architects, Los Angeles, USA, 2005. In response to an invitation to exhibit work on one column of a Los Angeles design gallery, Annie Chu and Rick Gooding chose to feature models of most of their projects to date. The resulting amalgamation collides scales, materials and orientations, and is, itself, a new work, a plastic collage that might suggest new ways of working. An uninterrupted 'modelscape', this is a contemporary three-dimensional version of Gandy's 'Public and Private Buildings' of Soane

A model as artwork exceeds the standard function of representing a building to be built. It becomes a way of functioning as an art object and is matched commercially and aesthetically by the preparedness of the art world to recognise models as artwork, to be commodified and sold. Architects' models have been displayed in galleries such as Max Protetch's gallery in Manhattan. At the Downtown Gallery, Leo Castelli auctioned models alongside artwork *as* artwork. Part of the reason so few models, particularly those by well-known Modern architects, are preserved in museums or other institutional collections is due to their popularity in the marketplace; most of these are collected by architects themselves. Artists' use of models often features as sculpture and multi-media pieces. A forerunner of this type, Marcel Duchamp's *Boîte-en-valise*, recasts previous art projects as a collection of limited edition miniatures assembled in a box. Meant to be displayed as a portable museum with special armatures and folding panels, *Boîte-en-valise* is a model gallery.

Other models are folded into other art circuits. Rather than looking to represent a building, these models are looking sideways to other art practices, painting and sculpture. Take, for example, El Lissitzky's two-dimensional representations which invite themselves to be experienced as representations of models or invitations to make a model. Here, via a new circuit, pictorial representation is reintroduced, not of a building, but of an elementary model expressed in three-dimensional *Prouns*, which El Lissitzky called 'transit stops for architecture'. These small-scale pieces widely influenced the Constructivists and the Bauhaus along with Malevich's *Arkitektons* and Tatlin's early wall-reliefs. Zaha Hadid's architectural career springs from these. Just as with El Lissitzky, Hadid's models cycle through pictorial information. Models as artwork flit between three- and two-dimensional representation; freed from what might be called conventional model functions, they come to the gallery either as model-sculpture or as model-photographs. Model/art crossover work is seen in the contemporary work of artists like Ron Mueck, Julian Opie, Peter Garfield, Oliver Boberg, Thomas Demand, Christoph Draeger, Thomas Hirschhorn, Jake and Dinos Chapman, Ben Langlands and Nikki Bell.

Food

In a quest to collect models – either as toys, souvenirs or art objects – the climax of any sequence of consumption must run to consumption in the literal sense, eating the model. Two obvious examples of model-food, the gingerbread house and wedding cake, both feature as ceremonial objects at special occasions. Originally published in 1812 by the Brothers Grimm, *Hansel and Gretel* describes a small edible house. The tale puts two lost children in a dark forest alone and hungry until they come upon a small house, *"built completely of bread and covered with cake with the windows of pure sugar"*.[15] Allen Weiss points out, *"This wish fulfillment, this extreme oral gratification, temporarily assuaging the terror of being abandoned, in fact veils an even greater and more primal fear: that of being devoured."* [16] In successive versions of the story, including Humperdinck's ballet, the Grimms' story is elaborated; the house becomes a gingerbread house studded with every conceivable confectionery. Like wedding cakes, gingerbread houses became popular during the Victorian age. The association was so strong that Victorian architecture is referred to as Gingerbread.

The first tiered wedding cake, so the legend goes, was prepared by a London baker [in] Fleet Street. This reinvention of the bridal cake was modelled on the steeple of – what else – nearby St Bride's church; one of many City churches designed by Sir Christopher Wren after

Left
Swiss cheese plate for
architects. Designed by Ryan
Fujita, cheese and toast are
assembled as the Villa Savoye
by Le Corbusier

the Great Fire. The poet, WE Henley wrote of its *"fanciful, formal, finicking charm"* and described it as *"that madrigal of stone"*. The cake version might never have caught on so well had it not later received the royal seal of approval of Queen Victoria's daughters who chose tiered cakes for their wedding receptions. These majestic cakes were several feet tall and clearly made reference to the object of their inspiration with pilasters and swags. The wedding cake's symbolic function – to make reference to the churchly site of the ceremony and thereby connect the celebration with the ceremony that precedes it – still persists even when the ceremony takes place elsewhere.

No one better epitomised the architectural ambitions of the chef than Marie-Antoine Carême who served Napoleon, Czar Alexander I and George IV. His trademark was to produce desserts resembling architectural models. These *pièces montées* could take the form of iced temples on meringue mountains or palaces in marzipan with candied fruit tree orchards surrounding them. Others resembled rustic mills with a moving wheel and champagne sluice. Carême, considered the father of French cooking and the inventor of Proust's madeleine, wrote cookery treatises like *L'Art Culinaire* and *Le Patissier Pittoresque* taking inspiration from architects like Vignola and Durand rather than other chefs, declaring that the main branch of architecture within the fine arts was confectionery.

Peter Wheelwright and Laurie Simmons

The Kaleidoscope House 2000

The Kaleidoscope Designer Doll House has design ambitions far exceeding the average toy. Designed by architect Peter Wheelwright, Chair of Architecture at Parsons School of Design, and artist Laurie Simmons, it is a scale model (1 inch = 1 foot) that breaks nearly every stylistic rule of doll's housing. An open plan with interchangeable coloured transparent sliding partitions, the white plastic house is unapologetically Modern.[1] Miniature furniture and decoration for the house are specially designed by real architects and artists: Dakota Jackson, Karim Rashid, Ron Arad, Peter Halley, Cindy Sherman and Mel Kenduck, Jon Newman, Barbara Kruger and Michael Graves.

Its collaborator is the Vitra Museum, known for costly miniatures of its sizeable chair collection. Nobody is fooled when the doll's-house is advertised for ages six and up; the Kaleidoscope House is really pitched to adults. Featured in *The New York Times, The Washington Post, House and Garden* and *Architecture* it is criticised as if it were a full-scale architectural project. On display at the London Design Museum, it is a model that can be purchased and taken home to houses that can never hope to equal this new toy. Here is a chance to own an expressly built gallery of limited editions where the 'signature building' itself becomes a piece of sculpture in your sitting room. This is a model as the ultimate consumable.[2]

Looking past the colours and the plastic furniture, the Kaleidoscope House is reminiscent of another house lodged in the memories of many architects, and the only model featured in *Towards a New Architecture*.

"His Citrohan house model of 1921 was the thorough expression of a conception of architecture as radical technically as Gropius' factory and as novel aesthetically as Oud's village. The enormous window area and the terraces made possible by the use of ferroconcrete, together with the asymmetry of the composition, undoubtedly produced a design more thoroughly infused with a new spirit, more completely freed from the conventions of the past than any thus far completed."[3]

In plan, section and massing, the Kaleidoscope House makes reference to Le Corbusier's prototype house. This 'hip' new doll's-house is some 80 years old! The double-height living room and overlooking balcony, dining room and bedroom placement are identical in both – even the grand piano featured in Le Corbusier's plan finds correspondence in the toy. The unusually placed

Below
This side elevation view of the
Kaleidoscope House is close
to the angle of a renowned
photograph of Le Corbusier's
Maison Citrohan model. The
section of the living room
versus the rest of the house
is clearly shown

Above
The sliding plastic panels of
the elevation start to overlap
and sponsor secondary
colours in an Op Art fashion

entry door located on the side of the Citrohan
House is similarly placed in the Kaleidoscope
House. The only marked difference between the
houses is the curved rather than the flat half-storey
at the top and the transfer of the hearth from the
back of the Citrohan House to the front of the
Kaleidoscope House. The transparent partitions
open the doll's-house from all sides (as opposed to
the rear facade access in traditional doll's-houses),
these partitions also take a cue from Le Corbusier's
playful wall of fenestration at the front of Citrohan.

Here is an example of a toy emulating a model
and certainly models have been mistaken for or
treated like toys. Parallels between a doll's-house
and a house in the Modernist canon reinforce a
perception (obvious to anyone but architects sometimes) that models can seem toy-like. Models are
intelligible to the layperson in part because we
have all been conditioned to read models through
toy play as children. The charm of a scale model
partly rests with nostalgia, not an architectural
nostalgia forhistoricist styles, but nostalgia for
childhood in general. The Kaleidoscope House is
only one more forceful example of this association,
shared to varying degrees by other toys, other
models. Building blocks and other toy construction
sets take this association to its obvious conclusion:
all children are architects-in-training. Some lose
interest, others channel that interest professionally.

Right
This view highlights the bed-
rooms and access to the
clerestory space. Note the
authentic Le Corbusier furniture in the living room

Greg Lynn

Alessi Coffee and Tea Towers 2001-3

To mark the twentieth anniversary of its Tea and Coffee Piazza project, the Alessi company commissioned 20 architects to produce new designs. All are beautiful, but Greg Lynn's stands out for a number of reasons, many related to notions of prototype and model. Unlike most, Lynn's tea and coffee service does not distil his own signature architectural motifs as a pattern to manipulate coffeepot, teapot, milk jug or sugar bowl.

The vessels that compose his set are not deviations from some standard service based on some fetishised aspect of built or unbuilt work. Rather, Lynn, it would seem, transfers so many models of a given architectural project, perhaps his Embryological House, directly into Alessi's world of objects. The scale need hardly change here, many of his scale models are already the right size for a tea and coffee service. Four pod-like forms nestle round a hot water vessel, all these in turn fit in a reversible tray that looks just like a laser-cut site model, a landscape of little hills and valleys.

The technology employed in Lynn's Coffee and Tea Towers manufacture borrows from techniques used in the production of stealth bombers. Vacuum formed from paper-thin sheets of titanium, the objects can be read as magically hardened paper models. The vessels themselves are there-fore neither milled nor cast, but their formwork is. Each piece of formwork for any given vessel is only used a dozen times or fewer, so each ensemble of vessels, each tea and coffee set is unique. The formwork is another sort of model in and of itself, another site that sponsors limited editions. The formwork relies on the best model-making technology available while the set derived from that formwork relies on technology only recently deregulated by the military.

The technological savvy of Lynn's set links it mechanically with his architectural ambitions just as the design for the Coffee and Tea Towers links conceptually. Irregular but smooth surfaces, dove-tailing organic form with cutting-edge industrial processes, has been part of Lynn's vision for a long time; he used to map the surface of potatoes. Understandably, such a vision is costly and hard to fashion in terms of construction in the field. Lynn cannily uses the Alessi commission to test a model for some future building. This is achieved largely because the computer-aided manufacture techniques do not need to differ so much from one scale to the next.

Similar processes govern how a model might be crafted with a CNC routing machine and how components for an interior or a facade or a whole

Right

The complete Coffee and
Tea Tower ensemble clusters
as a bud in its stored position

Below

A series of vessels as yet
singular, each with its own
formal characteristics, already
suggests the texture and
profile of the Alessi project

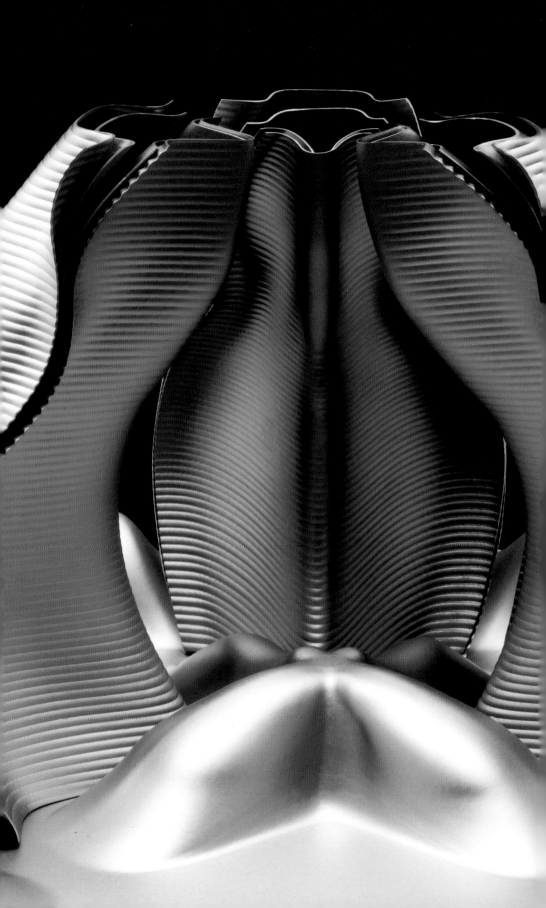

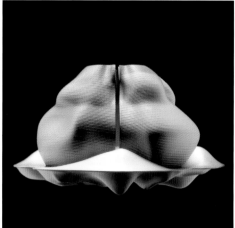

building might now be put together. Given this
reflexivity, it only makes sense to allow the Alessi
set to be a model and vice versa, just as a model
can be a building under these high-tech circumstances. Everything here is a model in some way.
That is why Lynn can honestly point to his Alessi
Tower and say it is the most architectural thing he
has yet done in his career.

The bespoke aspect of Lynn's Towers runs
together qualities of the hand-crafted and the
mechanised. If we think of Wedgwood and the
rest, tea sets have long been organised by a set
pattern, that is, by their non-uniqueness, even in
an age where consistency in manufacture was no
small feat. Indeed, tea sets presaged an aspiration
of the industrial revolution: ruthless consistency. So
Lynn's desire to bring architecture into a realm of
sensitive recalibration, where one size does not fit
all, spills into his Alessi project in a curious way.
Whereas low-tech tea sets are identical, his set is
not, thanks to the digital process. This is no real
victory for tea sets, but one for architectural form
in the shape of a series of models pretending to
serve tea and coffee.

Ben Langlands and Nikki Bell

Logo Works #1 1990
Millbank Penitentiary 1994
Marseille 2001

If there are artist's artists, there might also be architect's artists. Langlands and Bell would be exemplary in such a role. Their work is not so much architectural per se as it is about the architectural model and its conventions. Most of their projects, their 'sculptures', take the form of relief models that extrude a single plan or facade. These pieces abide by Alberti's dictum to render models monochromatically. What's more, in their preference to reveal a plan layer rather than the whole mass or exterior of a building, the projects nicely illustrate another model concept from Alberti:

"Between the design of the painter and that of the architect, there is this difference, that the painter by the exactness of his shades, lines and angles, endeavours to make the parts seem to rise from the canvas, whereas the architect, without any regard to the shades, makes his reliefs from the design of his platform, as one that would have his work valued, not by apparent perspective, but by the real compartments founded upon reason." [1]

Langlands and Bell are clearly mining this difference between painter and architect. Intense images are generated (many projects are photographed and sold as limited edition prints) that are all about light, shadow and perspective derived from simply shooting the scale relief model.

The subject matter is key to reading the work. The sculpture is not derived from invented plans, but specific precedents. *Millbank Penitentiary* is

a relief plan of the prison that used to occupy the site of Tate Britain gallery overlooking the Thames in London.

"Millbank Penitentiary embodies many paradoxes: the flower like formality of the punitive plan, and the journey from Old World penal institution to modern day art gallery. The role of Tate, like most art galleries, is arguably to manipulate and control art. The works are split up in much the same way as the Millbank prisoners, categorised, and treated differently in each section. Visitors are processed through the galleries by prescribed routes, while receiving a particular set of experiences. The final irony is the high level of social constraint imposed. In order to maintain control, certain rules are applied. Throughout the galleries the visitor route is monitored. The whole visit is surveyed." [2]

Logo Works #1 is a series of extruded plans or models of typical floors taken from the company headquarters of BMW, Unilever and the like. These white models are photographed and printed on fields of primary colour, using scale and architecture as corporate icons or 'modern heraldry'. Even the prints reveal the plans' sense of containment; isolation against the colour ground. Their orientation on the wall makes the headquarters into so many ant farms.

Marseille works backwards from the other projects in terms of technique. This sculpture is based on the artists' photograph of Le Corbusier's

Left

Marseille, wood, aluminium, glass, lacquer, 102×200×10 cm, 2001. The facade of Le Corbusier's Unité d'Habitation is conceived as a shallow relief in a dynamic perspective (a fly's-eye view).

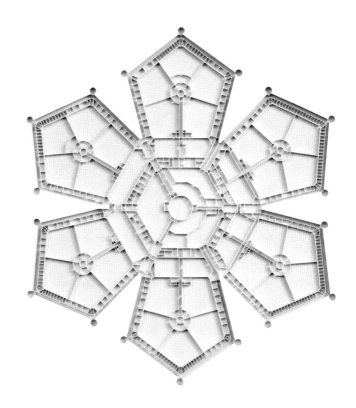

Right

Millbank Penitentiary, 1994

Right
Unilever, Hamburg

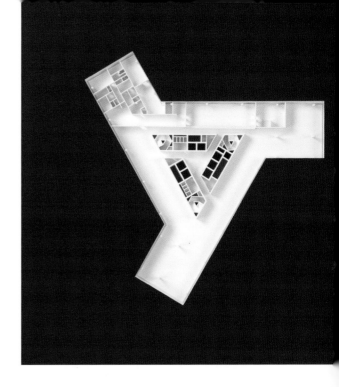

Below
BMW, Munich

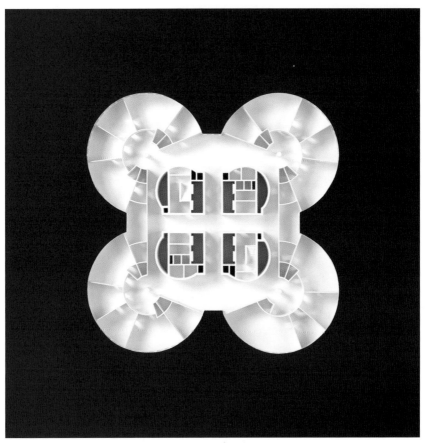

Architecture and the Miniature

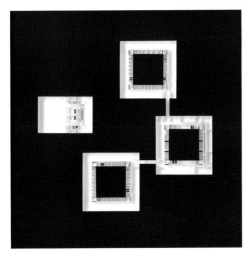

Above
IBM, Stuttgart

Unité d'Habitation apartment block. Thus, it is modelled in the particular perspective offered by the camera. The grid facade becomes inflected and reoriented, conjuring vertigo. All these artworks gain something in their fidelity to specific architectural projects as opposed to representing generic types. The texture of the work, its visual weight, is rooted in the details, the idiosyncrasies of the plans the models magnify. The display of these pieces is another aspect of the work in general. Special frames, armatures and vitrines stipulate the objects' claim to the gallery rather than the architect's office.

The level of craft exhibited by the work is also part of their qualification as art; they exceed any architect's requirements of exactitude. Their perfection as objects, what the artists refer to as their 'immaculate' quality, does not necessarily rule out their qualification as models, but allies them with final or competition models where some definitive image is sought. The focus on a single floor and the absence of site also erode their interpretation as workaday models and nudges them into some other camp, perhaps art.

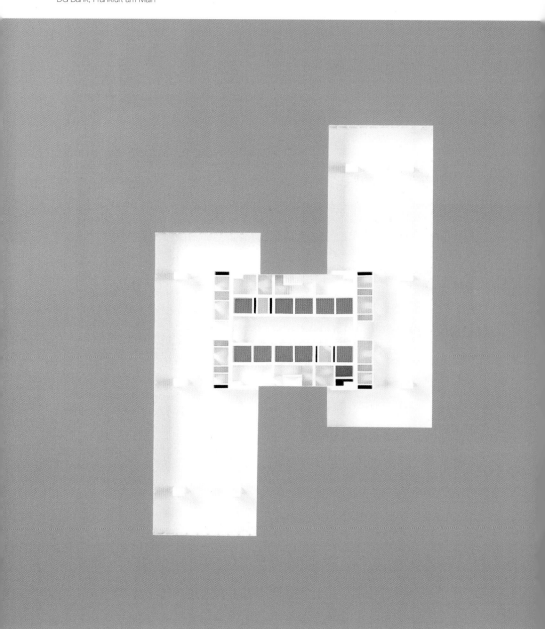

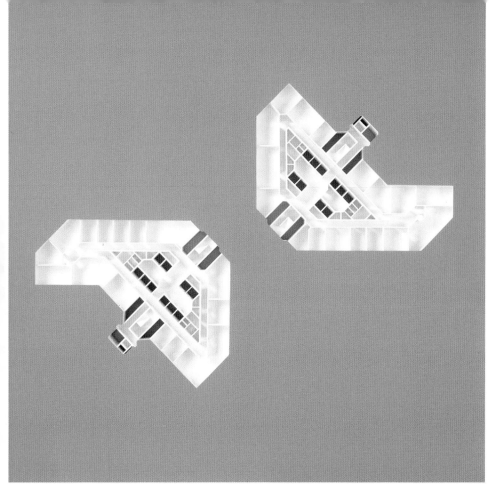

Above
Deutsche Bank, Frankfurt am Main

Opposite, above and **right**
Logo Works #2, (all of wood,
paint, lacquer and glass, 90 x
90 x15 cm), 1990. The link
between corporate icon and
architecture is usually seen in
some stylisation of a building's
facade or profile in a skyline.
Here the artists, Langlands
and Bell, reinvent this pairing
by focusing attention on the
building's plan and its prosaic
interior (office partitions, service
cores, structural bays). This is
anti-monumental and reveals
corporate culture, the environment of employees is offered
up as the defining aspect of
this reconfigured identity

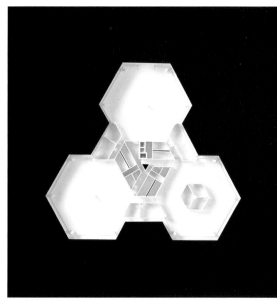

Above
Rank Xerox, Düsseldorf

Bekonscot Model Village

Bekonscot Model Village, Beaconsfield, Buckinghamshire, UK 1929

Britain abounds in model villages, diminutive townscape representations that appear in the countryside or at beach resorts as curiosities. Such things usually owe their genesis to eccentrics who start and cannot stop whittling the world down to size. Some of these are unstintingly true to their locale, others only tangentially so. The smallest towns boast the best model villages as objects of easy inspiration and complete fidelity.

A well-known example where the Queen celebrated her eighth birthday, Bekonscot Model Village was the pastime of a London accountant, Roland Callingham, who moved from Ascot to Beaconsfield and combined notions of both places in his extravagant hobby. It was not meant to represent accurately a specific place, but set out to encapsulate a particular time, pre-war Britain. Bekonscot boasts mini-rivers, lakes, a model railway and hundreds of buildings (all at a scale of 1:12) from urban to agrarian all in an effort to represent an England of yesteryear. The result of seventy-five years of modelling is a delightful Lilliputian suburban sprawl: Bekonscot covers 40,000 square feet, all outdoors, and includes some 1200 feet of scale train track.

The illusion fostered by places like Bekonscot is handled by a careful combination of natural and built elements; though even the *natural* is highly controlled. The planting in the foreground is heavily tended – Bonsai everything – so that views neatly

Right
High season at Bekonscot Model Village. Begun in 1929, this model metropolis continues to develop and attract interest

fuse with full-scale trees and shrubbery in the distance. Children stalk the village like creatures from a science fiction film. Bekonscot uses kinetic effects to register tempor-ality: the windmill, aero-drome, the tiny circus rides and the many trains (all marked BMR) are part of its scalar theatre. *"BMR stands for Bekonscot Model Railway and, as an independent line, the railway uses its own liveries, names and numbers."* Gaston Bachelard would approve: *"In looking at a miniature, unflagging attention is required to integrate all the detail."* [1] Many of the buildings comprising the village have precedent in Beaconsfield, Ascot or other places of interest like Hampton Court.

The only thing wrong with Bekonscot is its popularity. If too many people are visiting some of the illusion is lost. These places really require emptiness if one wants to move beyond the obvious King Kong illusion in favour of one that assumes a omniscient view of a real full-scale village lost in time. This requires lying down on the ground and squinting with one eye. There is an odd moment at Bekonscot – what Roland Barthes would call its punctum – where halfway through your journey there is a 4-foot granite obelisk featured inside a miniature racecourse. This by itself is not so strange, there were obelisks in the Circus Maximus. On it is mounted a memorial plaque to Callingham. Could this be his gravestone in the midst of kiddieland? Callingham gave all proceeds from the village to the Church Army which still manages the attraction today.

Above
Princess Elizabeth visits the village in 1934. Few can get this close to the models these days

Opposite
Background elements can help or hinder the illusion. As for the boy and girl, they might be giants

Mike McCrary

Mike's Amazing Cakes, Seattle, Washington, USA   2002

The opportunity to eat an architectural model is a strange one, especially for an architect. Consider, for example, those building dedication ceremonies where a cake in the form of the finished building is served. While it might be a novelty for everyone else, the architect is put in the position of taking part in a mock ruination of his/her design at the moment of its completion. Cakes have long been put in the service of this sort of representation.

The French chef, Marie-Antoine Carême, became famous for his elaborate pastries shaped into classical temples, palaces, pastoral scenes and gardens. This 'king of chefs and chef of kings' asserted in culinary treatises, 'The main branch of confectionery is architecture'. Jelly is another food-stuff easily cast into miniature wobbling buildings; Greg Lynn is a fan of the 1950s science-fiction thriller *The Blob* which features a building-sized jelly intent on destroying an American town. Ice creams and chilled desserts can also spoof architecture and provide the scalar thrill of eating representations of the built environment. Marcel Proust writes of the delight of finding Vendôme Columns in chocolate at the Ritz and considers a range of other edible models through the character of Albertine:

"As for ices (for I hope that you won't order one that isn't cast in one of those old-fashioned moulds which have every architectural shape imaginable), whenever I take one, temples, churches, obelisks, rocks, it is like an illustrated geography-book which I look at first of all and then convert its raspberry or vanilla monuments into the coolness of my throat [...] I set my lips to work to destroy, pillar by pillar, those Venetian churches of a porphyry that is made with strawberries, and send what's left over crashing down upon the worship-pers. Yes, all those monuments will pass from their stony state into my inside which throbs already with their melting coolness." [1]

Gingerbread is perhaps the most solidly architectural of foods. From the Grimm version to Martha Stewart's holiday structures, the ginger-bread house is a Victorian import from Germany. The fact of the matter is that ginger-bread houses are not really for eating so much as looking at and dreaming about eating (or being eaten if you're Hansel or Gretel). This edible model has entered popular culture. In a *Simpsons* episode, Homer Simpson tries to rescue his children caught in the fairytale.

Right

Gingerbread houses tend to
only look delicious. Architectural ambitions overshadow
the culinary

Below

Mike McCrary's amazing cake
of Craigdarroch Castle in
British Columbia, where the
groom proposed

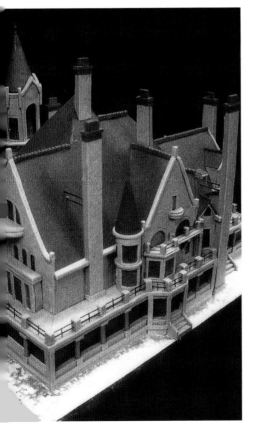

Homer: *Mmmm ... sugar walls.*

Lisa: *Father! I knew you'd rescue us!*

Homer: *Rescue you, stuff myself with candy,
it's all good!*

Witch: *Oh, that's a load bearing candy cane!
You clumsy oaf!*

Mike McCrary at Mike's Amazing Cakes has
revived the Carême tradition, offering highly accurate
model-cakes for events and weddings. Working
from photographs or blueprints, McCrary creates
skyscrapers, mansions and famous landmarks in
layers of biscuit, sponge and buttercream. These
might signify where a company has established a
new headquarters building or where a groom has
proposed.

Michael Cadwell

Pastoral Quartet   1995

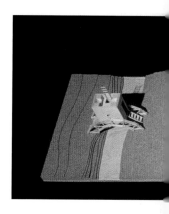

Architecture/art crossover work does not have to reside in the gallery. A series of small buildings designed and built by Michael Cadwell play with notions of categorisation and scale. Sited in parks as 'public sculpture', the built structures that comprise the Pastoral Quartet were first modelled in a particular way. Cadwell, an educator as well as an architect, crafted each model in basswood on sites composed of cork on a square backing of hardwood. The model structures each represent a hybrid or twinned building type: Ark-tower, Bridge-box, Drum-barge, House-tunnel. Much of the architectural interest for Cadwell is held in how these types are tectonically linked. Each has a distinct relationship to the landscape made evident in the models. One bridges, one floats, one towers, one buries itself in a hillside. All work with basic geometries. Cylinders, cubes and 45 degree pitched roofs play out across the four projects.

The models for the Pastoral Quartet are a project in their own right. They are made in such a way as to seem autonomous and capable of representing the intent of the author without regard to their intended use as three-dimensional templates for larger iterations. Much of this quality stems from the four models' shared scale, level of

craft and material palette. They invite speculation upon but do not clearly reveal reasons why they have been so grouped. Each model structure can be manipulated to reveal something hidden. In the case of the House-tunnel model, half the site model slides off to show the subterranean hall connecting the two separate elements poking above ground. This, in itself, is not an unusual model device, but with these models, the careful rendering of interiors seems to shift the project from the conventional to the symbolic. These little interiors are a revelation.

Many of the qualities sensed with these models are also held by the built work. The tension of the foursome available in the models is, however, absent as the hybrids are built apart at sites removed from one another. Nonetheless, the individual components of the quartet retain some-thing of their model presence. They are, after all, small buildings; their smallness only fully sensed once viewed in the landscape. You might say that these small buildings are equally large models.

The fact that the built work registers as somewhat under-scaled (relative to the covered bridges, guard towers, silos and so on) allows the small buildings to harness some benefits of the miniature. The built versions do not dominate but empower the viewer. They suggest forts and fantasies of childhood. They make reference to follies placed in the landscape as architecture

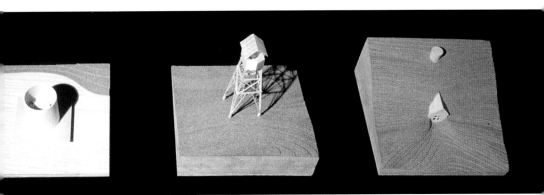

Above

The four models of the
Pastoral Quartet assembled,
each dealing with a different
site condition (stream, hill,
lake or field) and a different
typological hybrid

without obvious programme, as markers of some
larger narrative to be harvested by the viewer.
Another definition for a folly is, *"a building that
appears to be something other than what it is"*.[1]

Despite the distance between them, the
quartet recombines as photographs exhibited side
by side with the models. Each seems to justify the
other. The built structures validate the exactitude of
the models. The models guarantee the structures
were not built ad-hoc. The models further claim
that the four structures were conceived as parts
of a whole dedicated to a common purpose. The
project was a reaction against representation,
including model representation. Cadwell, like many
architects, had become frustrated with working
several degrees removed from actual building,
*"the abstractions of modelling, drawing and writing
about architecture became meaningless to me
when I no longer knew to what these abstractions
referred"*.[2] The Pastoral Quartet was intended as
a sensual, anti-intellectual self-education. So the
models Cadwell built were of a special order, not
crafted as precious objects but as necessary
stoppages focused on manifestation over pure
representation.

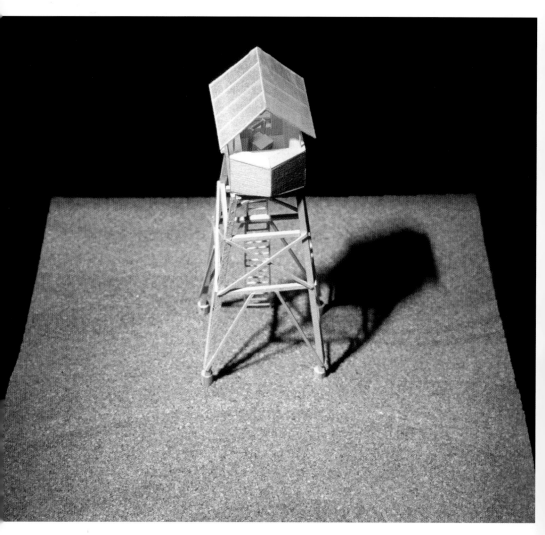

Above
The Ark-tower model introduces a new material to the
basswood and cork set

Opposite
House-tunnel invites the
viewer to lift the roof and view
the interior link between the
two elements

Architecture and the Miniature

Right
The model for the Bridge-box
project indicated scale with
the stair and ladder.

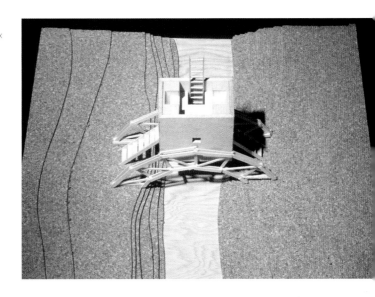

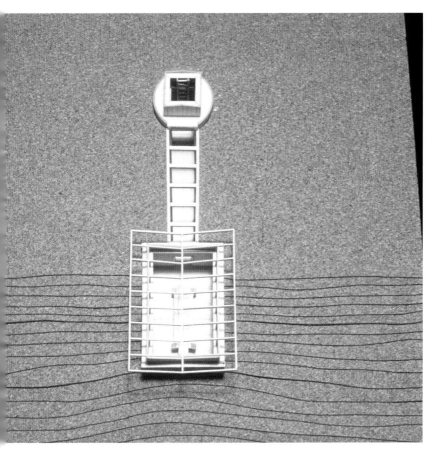

Interview with Gene Rizzardi

Hollywood Models 1990–2003

Responsible for award-winning effects in such films as *Titanic, Godzilla, X-Men,* and *Apollo 13,* legendary cinematic model maker Gene Rizzardi discusses his craft.

What educational or professional qualifications led you to your current work with models, effects and the film industry? How long have you been in business?

I have a degree in Commercial Art I got back in 1972 at New York Community College; I also studied industrial patternmaking and took a few semesters of photography. When I was in the service I learned how to fix typewriters and Xerox machines. I have built models since I was twelve, mostly cars, aeroplanes and boats. When I was in my teens I started reading model aeroplane magazines and found I had a great interest in radio control models, here is where I started building real skills. I also helped build a home for my grandparents and picked up basic woodworking and painting skills. And I have been building models professionally now for about 27 years.

What are the typical logistics of your trade? Do you build most models in your studio or on location near film production? Do you keep a regular model crew to assist you?

Most movie model work is based on a per project situation. Sometimes I am called into an existing shop to lead or be part of a crew building models for a specific movie, television show or commercial. On other projects, the production company decides it would like to build all the models in-house. A facility is found that will allow the building and photographing of the miniatures and we set up a shop. We rent or purchase all the equipment, build the desks, work tables, storage rooms, have the phones put in and the Internet and start building. We are usually given no more than two weeks to get ready, and when the show is over, everything goes into storage or is sold.

As a member of both the Association for Professional Model Makers (APMM) and the Visual Effects Society, do you often work with architects?

The APMM has architects in the membership, the Visual Effects Society has production designers or art directors that may have been architects at one time. Within the motion picture industry (and on my staff) I have hired architectural model makers to assist in the construction of cityscapes and landscapes.

In your role at the Academy of Motion Picture Arts and Sciences, is there debate about the status of physical versus computer models? Do the Academy Awards recognise the difference?

Preparations are made for a
tracking shot along a model
of Park Avenue for the film
Godzilla

In the Academy, we base our awards on the
best visual effect, we do not specify whether it is
physical or digital. In the Visual Effects Society we
award 20 different categories, and Best Models
and Miniatures is one category, today this can be
either a digital or a physical model. This category
is difficult to describe since today most models of
landscapes or cityscapes have digital set extensions
or added digital effects, like smoke, rain, water,
haze and even explosions.

*Do you feel there is a future for straight scale
models (as opposed to digital) within special
effects cinema? What are the advantages of
using tangible models in film?*

In just about every Academy Award-winning
special effects movie you will find a mix of digital
and physical models. There are very few 'straight'
model shots any more since you can modify and
enhance a shot. Also many backgrounds are
added later, and most films go through a digital
editing process today and that is where even a
'straight' shot can be modified. Do we still need
physical models? I believe there is nothing like
them, and when shot properly, they are cheaper
than a digital model. You only have to look at
movies like *Lord of the Rings, King Kong*, and *Star
Wars* to see the use of models and miniatures is
not a dead art.

Left
Park Avenue in Manhattan is given the model treatment by Rizzardi. This straight shot includes detritus from a battle at street level. Care is taken to not let the buildings look too new with the addition of graffiti, pollution stains and boarded windows. Digital atmospheric effects augment the model scene in the film

Opposite
Models and marionettes are the focus of *Team America* (from the creators of South Park), where Rizzardi created sections of a miniature Paris, full of abbreviated monuments and visual puns – the streets are paved with croissants

Below
While most projects require Rizzardi to gather a team and create a makeshift workshop on-site, occasionally models can be crafted in his studio. This view shows the backs of buildings to be used in the film *Godzilla*

In films you've worked on like Titanic, Godzilla, Mighty Joe Young *or* Honey, I Blew Up the Kids, *architectural models meet destruction. Are you also in charge of the pyrotechnics? How is this typically achieved?*

When we are going to blow up the model for a shot, my job is to prep the model by constructing it to break realistically. I do have a pyrotechnic licence, but I don't have a high enough classification to be in charge of designing the explosives. I am permitted to help load and have pushed the button when the time comes to trigger the effects.

Academic training specifically tailored for model makers is a recent invention (you can now find degree-granting programmes across the globe). Do you feel the field is set to grow beyond the demands of Hollywood? What advice would you offer aspiring model makers?

The skills you learn as a scale model maker transfer well into the digital world if needed. With the lack of woodwork shops and machine shops in many of our nation's junior and high schools, we are endangering our future. If someone pulled the plug, how would we make anything?

Are our schools churning out too many model makers?

Maybe for Hollywood, but there are museum models, architectural models and prototypes to be made and all require the same basic skill set that a model maker has to offer. Many of the top model makers are in their fifties and sixties so we will be retiring soon and we need replacements to keep the business vibrant.

My advice to anyone considering a career in model making is to learn how to build a model physically *and* digitally. Learn to use the traditional tools (tablesaw, bandsaw, sanders, drillpress, etc.) and learn how to program a CNC milling machine or CNC router. If you can master all of this you will be formidable and in high demand. This is a business that will get into your blood, in your hair and under your fingernails.

Virtual Estimations of CAD

"The computer in the design studio provokes both extravagant claims and high levels of anxiety." With this Stan Allen acknowledges both the delight and trepidation architects associate with the digital. He also cautions not to discount the computer despite the hyperbole and science fiction surrounding it: "The luddite option, for all of its rhetorical attractiveness, is untenable, and, finally, uninteresting. What is required is to become familiar enough with the technology so as to be able to strip away its mythological veneer." [1] A luddite aficionado of the scale model could say that the computer has undone the model, traded the real for the virtual and by doing so depleted modelling – and therefore architecture – in the process.

We know this is not the case. Certainly computer-aided design (CAD)[2] has dramatically changed the education and profession of architects. But what was traded or transformed from the start was not the model so much as the drawing.

> The use of the computer in the design studio has facilitated two important shifts in design practice that have yet to be examined critically. First is a renewed use of perspectives, which once had to be laboriously drawn by hand but can now be generated effortlessly by clicking a button. Second is the use of colour. Colour in the computer is either extravagantly false or attempts to simulate photographic representation of reality through sophisticated rendering programs incorporating reflection, transparency and texture mapping. In both cases, the ease of achieving seductive effects has as yet overwhelmed any impulse to question the relationship between the means of representation and the architectural intention.[3]

In the early 1980s the computer's architectural application was centred on mapping and plotting plans; picture those big machines with pivoting stylus arms. By the late 1980s so much had changed. The machines shrank, the mouse became standard equipment and it

Right
Interior view down a hallway.
Here the effects exceed the
requirements of the representation. The student wishes to
broadcast the sensibility of
the project even in secondary
spaces and this is afforded by
the software which does not
presume a hierarchy of form

wasn't enough just to digitise blueprints, the model would be next. Several software packages would be introduced to offer virtual modelling, one of the forerunners and still one of the most popular was a program devised by an academic in Ohio. Since the 1990s, computer-aided manufacture (CAM) has made it possible to translate computer designs into three-dimensional forms either milled or topographically layered from a given material.

Architecture A to Z

The virtual model first reached a broad-based market in 1989 with the launch of FormZ, modelling software developed at the Ohio State University and incorporated a year later as a private company, Automatic Design Systems. While there had already been CAD products in the market for several years, these were often large, expensive, highly specialised programs requiring professional grade equipment and people trained to input coordinate data. In many ways the software that architects used prior to FormZ was largely concerned with digitising drawings making revisions simply a matter of reprogramming rather than redrafting. Computer-aided modelling was still rather primitive or nonexistent. FormZ changed all that. From its inception in the hands of its creator, Chris Yessios, FormZ strove to be cheap, easy and accessible. What is more, it did something no other program of that time was capable of: it digitally modelled with ease.

With FormZ, digital modelling is notionally a process of extrusion. Two-dimensional figures – squares, circles, polygons – are given a depth. These rudimentary virtual objects can then be joined together or manipulated. FormZ, marketed as 'the 3-D form synthesiser', offered a long list of possible operations: extrusions, sweeps, lathed objects, terrain modelling, Boolean operations, revolved and geodesic spheres, deformations, and object unfolding. Quite apart from other CAD packages, it allowed one to design notionally in virtual two and three dimensions simultaneously. The 'space' for these synthesised objects was a Cartesian

set of grids – height, width and depth – x, y and z. It was the depth, or the 'z' dimension, that made Form Z famous.[4]

Programs like FormZ suggested that the computer could design *for* you automatically. After describing a few extruded base objects geometrically, the program's list of manipulations could be enacted with a few keystrokes and certain operations or series of commands could transform objects beyond recognition. Immediate complexity was possible. So irresistible were those keystrokes that they can now be seen in all their possible variations with new buildings constructed across the globe. For a time, students using the new software appeared to produce more elaborate work in less time than practising architects. The sheer density of information printed from computer screens – the number of lines per square inch, the number of prisms welded together – initially overwhelmed critical response. Just the fact that these designs came from a computer rather than the hand seemed to promise precision, efficiency and premature professionalism.

The drafting capabilities of Form Z were rather limited compared with the sophisticated devices available in architects' offices. Form Z, unlike the others, was principally about modelling until recently it never tried to compete with the technical drawing applications already on offer. The media were quick to hail the program as revolutionary. In a few short years, FormZ was showcased in new computer laboratories in architecture schools across America, Canada and Europe – particularly in Britain. The computer lab became the expensive showpiece for many schools as proof of their budgetary vigour and technological edge. Form Z, requiring little in terms of equipment, permitted schools to offer so many more workstations. Not surprisingly, architecture schools rather than offices were initially attracted to Form Z. It would take a

generation of FormZ graduates installed in the workplace to persuade the profession to invest in such software. Hollywood was eager to use the system and lure architecture graduates away from their intended careers. FormZ was so successful so fast that, inevitably, many other competing software companies broke into the market with their own modelling packages.

Taken as a whole, CAD pre-tests a project in so many ways and across so many formats that the architectural product can be practically flawless. Unlike painters or sculptors who work directly with their medium, an architect typically operates remotely from real building. Traditionally, architectural design is relayed to the building trades through conventional drawings and models. This distance between the architect and the building has in many ways been mitigated with the advent of CAD systems. While the computer merely digitises the architectural drawing, the architectural model undergoes more obvious changes.

What was so new and revolutionary about FormZ? Absolutely nothing. Yessios reworked ideas that had always informed the tradition of architecture. The Cartesian 'space' of his program allowed designers to see on-screen sectional, oblique or perspective views of objects. With FormZ the illusion of three-dimensional space was achieved with rendering shadows on surfaces of objects, assuming a given light source; a good Renaissance skill. This, together with perspective views – another Renaissance trick available at the touch of a button – gave students an image that offered the illusion of looking at a real scale model. But, to be sure, this was never a model, it was a very effective drawing. FormZ offered an immediate sense of exactitude and finality from the start of the design process and the ability to render virtual objects not so much as models but as images of proto-buildings. In many ways CAD recreated the architectural photograph.

It is not difficult to pinpoint how CAD differs from traditional modelling in some respects. First, there is the question of size versus scale. One of the basic advantages of working with a computer model as opposed to the standard type is the ability to work in real dimensions. But in specifying the real size of model elements the notion of 'model' is somewhat undone. A model of full dimensions is either a 1:1 mock-up or, indeed, a building. True, most renderings and CAM models are printed to a scale, but the virtual model itself is technically full-scale even at its earliest stages. Why is this a problem? Consider that over the course of a project, analogue models tend to follow a route whereby they begin as scaleless sketch models and then, by stages, are built to more exacting and progressively larger scales. Scale enters the project bit by bit in line with the refinement of the design:

> The model clearly acquires a very important status. Up to now it has served mainly to deliver a miniature of the future building. But in virtual reality you can create models at a scale of 1:1. And as soon as you can build virtual spaces in which you can experience events that actually take place somewhere else, it will be possible to imagine the virtual model as a design tool of future architectural practice. This touches upon the question of mental images. I always try to make my students imagine their projects before drawing them. … What I ask them to do is in fact create nothing less than a mental virtual model.[5]

Such a thing recalls Arnheim's 'thought model', which he outlines as a conception made possible by scalar thinking or thinking in miniature as one of the abilities that defines the architect. Are 'mental virtual models' really 1:1? Does virtuality necessarily impose real size from the murky moment of a design's conception? Why wouldn't familiarity with a design tool (the computer) negate the need or desire to think outside that system, to think in miniature?

FormZ was distinctive because it permitted a kind of virtual sculpting; with both additive and subtractive processes. Forms can be grouped or melded or sliced. Before a form can be manipulated in this way, it is typically generated from a two-dimensional profile. This process recalls Alberti's notion of extrusion, of the model rising directly from the drawing. It might be difficult if not impossible to capture the sensibility of the folded paper model on the computer but other operations are offered.[6] The folded paper model was about sharing materiality with the drawing, playing with surface and using folded corners as a basis for the model's structure (in a simplistic mimicry of walls and floor plates). Few FormZ models are about pure surface; they are not so much paper as digital clay. It is impossible to discern an early versus a late FormZ model. There is usually one up-to-date version, an accretion or palimpsest of all the previous versions. In this, there is no virtual sketch model in the way it had been known. The first prism to be extruded at the start of a project is as perfect and immaterial as the last. In effect, everything in FormZ enjoys zero tolerance. How can a sketch operate within these parameters? A traditional modelling process involves a series of fragmented starts, some of which might be refined until one is pushed forward and rebuilt, this one being more accurate than the rest.

The traditional rebuilding of the project in a series of ever more refined models amounts to an architectural rehearsal. Redoing something again and again as opposed to updating or modifying something represents a marked difference between physical and virtual model

Right and below

Greg Lynn FORM, trial models for Alessi Coffee Tower. Lynn captures the distinct beauty of digital models in works big and small – indeed, these prototype forms for a new coffee service could be at any scale. Their complex geometry and striated surfaces would be difficult to capture with analogue techniques, but there is a crispness to these digital renderings that surpasses photographs of real objects

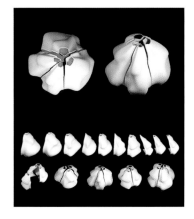

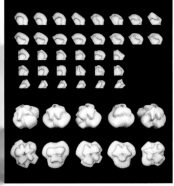

Bottom

The wire-frame model has its own visual appeal, offering simultaneous views of every surface. Spidery and intense, these are rarely featured as prime representations. Rather, despite their attractiveness, they are considered as merely a working step to rendered surface models

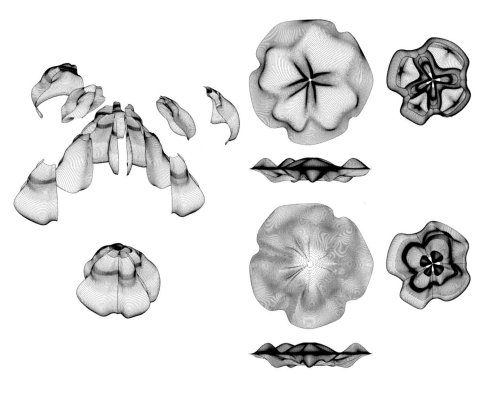

processes. The rehearsal of form in various materials to increasing levels of accuracy introduces either a commitment or a rethink each time. The model rehearsal requires the rebuilding of all elements, even those considered finished; this does not happen with the computer where only elements requiring revision need to be refashioned.

What of the accident in process? *"The promise here is that if computer technology can create more and more realistic simulations, design mistakes will be avoided."* [7] That's a problem if you desire mistakes. The accidents peculiar to the scale model take place in *"the distance interposed between the thing and its representation".* [8] That is to say, accidents forced or happenstance that are contingent to working to scale, in miniature; for example, a model falling to the floor. There are less dramatic accidents: the element glued upside down, the wall that tilted out of alignment. All these are the dividends of process. The computer can generate random forms or model operations set to wide parameters, but these aren't the same as the accident of the physical studio model. *"The interruption and the accident need to be cultivated; software systems might be used against the grain."* [9]

In terms of representation there is beauty in the latest CAD imagery, which can be delicate, translucent or complex. The main charge to level against CAD's representation has to do with its obvious flatness. Restricted to two dimensions on-screen, programs like FormZ compensate by offering more sophisticated texture maps, surfaces that resemble steel, glass and so on. This prompts what many critics have pointed to as a loss of abstraction in favour of intense realism at all stages of a project's development on the computer. The one thing the computer does not have – tangible three-dimensional form – programmers overcompensate for by offering unrelenting pictorial realism: *"One of the curious aspects of digital technology is the valorisation of a new realism. From Hollywood special effects to architectural rendering, the success of the new technology is measured by its ability to seamlessly render the real."* [10] As part of that realism, CAD favours interiority. The images and 'fly-throughs' characteristic of CAD project display overcome the god-like viewpoint common to looking at conventional scale models. Instead, what is offered is a sequence of interiors where the exterior works like a cinematic frame.

CAD does streamline things for the designer once one is beyond the sketch phase. But there is a question about its ability to communicate. Certainly, within schools of architecture or offices, mentors and peers are by now trained to 'see' CAD models and respond to them as fully-fledged designs. What had been a problem before – faculty or senior partners in a firm not understanding a design proposal represented on the computer – is fading. However, there are still problems of reception with a client or a public with no architectural training. The scale model therefore persists as a kind of universal representation, intelligible to non-architects. CAD drawings and renderings remain, like blueprints, professionally codified. Even this erodes as more people become familiar with digital simulations elsewhere: computer games, the Internet, film and TV.

The computer is good at archiving and representing existing stuff, mapping facades from photographs and so on. Authorial control of site is limited here, tweaking the site to suit the project is not so easy because the accurate site is provided. The common architectural trick of toning down the environment and detailing (cooking up) the proposal is compromised by programs like PhotoShop which encourage inserting the proposal (at the right perspective) into a photograph of the site. This ease of visibly suturing in a proposal mitigates the need for a

Above and **right**
Mirror effects and tile mapping
throughout tend to erode the
'pre-effects' version which is,
in fact, already loaded with
effects. The unlikely viewpoint
is also disturbingly evocative
of some hidden camera.

3-D site model at all. It is a question of conceptual memory versus the memory capacity of the computer. Abstraction tends to lose out.

Virtuality implies otherworldliness, that which Margaret Wertheim calls *"the medieval return of cyberspace, favouring mind over body to an extreme. Here contemporary dreams of cyberspace parallel the age-old Platonic desire to escape from the 'cloddishness' of the body into a 'transcendent' realm of disembodied perfection – the realm of the soul"*.[11] Analogue models, by contrast, seem to play up their physicality by virtue of their relationship to the body. *"Miniatures have a further feature. They are 'man made' and, what is more, made by hand. They are therefore not just projections or passive homologues of the object: they constitute a real experiment with it."*[12] Lévi-Strauss suggests that this in itself adds a 'supplementary dimension' to the model. *"Merely by contemplating it he is, as it were, put in possession of other possible forms of the same work; and in a confused way, he feels himself to be the creator …"*[13] With the case of the computer, even the designer (much less anyone else) may feel distanced in the creation of the model by a combination of exactitude and mechanical mediation. But what the computer model may deny in terms of authorship, it lends in control. A digitally fabricated model, however, would challenge this assumption:

> In this new architectural domain, joints just don't matter. (So, presumably, there are no Scarpas in cyberspace.) Surfaces have no thickness, and they can be fitted together with mathematical precision. You don't need nails, screws, or glue. There is no need to accommodate changes of material. Furthermore, there is no weather to keep out. In short, there is no room for ingenuity (or God) in the details; the game is entirely one of space and surface.[14]

Of course, a surface membrane can be as symbolically charged as anything else.

The paperless office or studio is invoked as one of the main advantages to be gained from modelling software and computers in general. The paperless studio, it is argued, promises a streamlined process. It is a minimalism that guards against clutter and cluttered thinking. Restricting the design process to the computer erases the need for or hides the evidence of false starts and changes. CAD programs take endless revision as a matter of course. One never sees the FormZ models that didn't work displayed as one would show sketch models. Who saves older versions of a digital model? The effort is not serial, it is one of continual tweaking and layers.

In this way a digital model never fails as a design, it simply grows in detail, reacts to new information. Rejected elements do not accumulate in the corner – they disappear or morph into correct forms. The rules of a computer lab (no food, no drink, no noise) reinforce a sensibility of hygiene that is associated with digital design.[15] FormZ models are clean, perfect and untouched. This suits the obsessive compulsive where the perfection of the virtual model is matched by the perfection of its means of production. There is no paper trail, no index of effort. Of course this breeds the fear that the model all too easily can be lost. A day's work, if not backed up, can be snatched away by a power failure or a computer malfunction. Constant back-up is required. Then there is the problem with theft, how easily the model's file can be copied, sent over the Internet.

Until recently the pleasures of the computer model, as Allen suggests, were bound to its display on the monitor or in printed renderings. The pleasure of specifying a viewpoint, pushing a button, and watching a perspective generate in seconds is meaningful to those mindful of the tedium of drawing accurate perspectives by hand. The addition of colour to these perspective views now recalls the definitive image of the Beaux-Arts: the dramatic tinted perspective. A series of perspectives can generate a 'fly-through' presentation inviting the architect into the realm of cinema. This prompts an endless desire for verisimilitude – realistic lighting, textures and reflections – so that the model might compete as a special effect. Digital models share their mode of display with television and film, creating the assumption that virtual models should compete with or mimic cinema:

> [I]t ignores what has traditionally given architectural representation its particular power of conceptualization – that is to say, its necessary degree of abstraction, the distance interposed between the thing and its representation.[16]

The digital model is compelled to be finished, to spoof not an architectural model, but often a photograph of a building. Its insistence on real scale is part of a sequence that forgoes a degree of abstraction in favour of representing the real. To summarise some main points regarding architectural models versus computer representations:

- Walter Benjamin claims that, *"buildings are appropriated in a two-fold manner: by use and by perception – or rather, by touch and sight"*.[17] These terms might also explain part of the difference between the architectural model and the computer simulation. The latter works for vision only, while the former also celebrates haptic materiality and the physical traces of the maker.
- The model celebrates the aura of the artist's hand and the Ruskinian idea of imperfection as the sign of life while the computer simulation revels in the mystique of machinic perfection and in the code of realism.
- Part of the illusion of realism is the oft-repeated but ultimately mistaken claim that computer drawings are in real scale. However, the representation is never really full size; it is that only virtually in the normal sense of the word, as when we talk about virtual force in physics.
- In a different sense, virtual reality representations are much less virtual than the traditional model. The traditional model allows for the serendipity of bricolage and the 'virtual' creativity of chance, while computer simulation is characterised, and often constrained by preformation and limitation.
- The rough model makes it clear that it is not the real thing, releasing a virtuality that can inspire the viewer to create something new (by transgressive actions, weird perspectives, reorganisation of parts), while the near-photographic realism of the computer representation celebrates spaces and surfaces (and suppresses tectonic joints, haptic qualities and so on), but simultaneously separates the viewer from the finished design that can be viewed but not touched.
- Like the aeroplane, the model gives the architect the *"implacable bird's-eye view"* that according to Le Corbusier is *"the superior expedient of modern planning"*.[18] The computer simulation makes interiors available to the inquisitive eye.
- The model emphasises the objectness of the building, making it an organic unity comparable to a work of sculpture, for example, while the elaborate perspectives and fly-through films made available by the computer emphasise the viewer and fragment the building into visual sequences.

Jawad al-Tabtaba'i

A Mosque for Dearborn, Michigan, USA   2005

As part of a thesis project focusing on Islamic architecture, student Jawad al-Tabtaba'i selected downtown Dearborn, the American city with the highest concentration of Muslims, as his site. His goal for the project was ambitious:

"Contemporary Islamic architecture has a tendency to either ignore its past and traditions or mimic them. Both approaches deprive the architecture of its richness and potentials. In an effort to understand the essence of Islamic architecture, modern building technology, materials and context need to be investigated as instruments of its expression. Furthermore, elements from Islamic culture such as Arabic calligraphy and carpet weaving, could become an opportunity to inform the architecture." [1]

To achieve this synthesis, al-Tabtaba'i worked from the start on the computer, using a range of modelling, drafting, layout and animation programs. Going digital straight away gave the student leave to produce three-dimensional models from the start. He could scan calligraphic art and use it as an underlay for digital modelling. He could also check the results in perspective under specific light conditions. Opportunities afforded by the computer to resize, repeat, attenuate and extrude any given pattern opened new venues that he took. A handful of forms once created could in turn be reworked and filter through the whole of the project – at the scale of the building, a single room, a piece of furniture – lending the design a distinct consistency. In essence, the student wove a limited number of forms together to generate a formally rich project. This would have been cumbersome, perhaps impossible, to achieve with an analogue model.

Another obvious benefit of the digital process in this case was that the interior of the mosque received equal, if not more, attention to the exterior. Experience of interior spaces, animated in full perspective from realistic viewpoints with accurate shadows, became the dominant way of looking at and designing the project. Rather than altering isometric views and checking how the result might appear in perspective, the student could easily manipulate the model in perspective and look at the impact of the change in plan or section afterwards. The texture, transparency and reflectivity of every surface were open to programming. Quite

Opposite
A view of the prayer hall, examining various light effects and surface textures

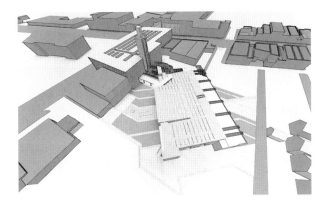

Right
A view of Jawad al-Tabtaba'i's mosque for Dearborn *in situ* near a prominent intersection. The mosque is accessed through and is located behind a disused department store

Opposite
An interior perspective shows the vestibule with access to the mezzanine. These views are intentionally black and white focusing attention where needed

Below
Not aiming at photorealism, al-Tabtaba'i renders figures as flat, translucent silhouettes. This is clearly a virtual model, not a virtual building

early on, certain views of the project appeared in a highly finished form, though this might not always have been a benefit.

If we consider the mindset of the designer, the ability to make what is a sketch model seem as if it is an advanced model view can upset the typical creative process. Owing to his facility with the modelling and rendering software, the student's project occasionally took on a false sense of completion, seeming over before it really began. This was an illusion, but the student had to overcome this by-product of the digital to progress and grapple with questions of structure, egress, vertical circulation and so on – all of which positively altered initial formal gestures.

Eventually the project organisation included well over a hundred different model 'layers' that the designer could turn on or off depending on the task. This forced the student to invent a complicated nomenclature to keep the layers straight in his own mind; a system of coded file names by no means apparent to anyone else.

At the point when his instructors required an analogue model, the project quickly revealed certain problems. First, the laser cutter available to follow the digital model can only cut planes rather than make true solids. This resulted in so many flat pieces to connect and glue together that the task became onerous. Second, the digital model, though appearing complete from certain viewpoints, in fact remained somewhat open-ended and unresolved. This complication prompted worthwhile changes to the digital model, making it more complete, but the physical model itself languished. To make up for this absence in documentation, al-Tabtaba'i instead composed a video sequence of the digital model.

Rather than the standard fly-through of a completed virtual model, the video showed the growth of the project, piece by piece, almost as if it had been conventionally crafted. He connected individual components of the mosque, the Mihrab for example, shown in the process of assembly. The video was an effective strategy and the overall design for the mosque took an award. Of all the representations of the project, it best conveyed the student's intent. Although the video did not require any real translation of the digital model, as the analogue model assignment did, crafting the video took as long, if not longer.

What is most interesting about the video is that for all its technical sophistication, its success lay in marrying the digital object to something like

an analogue process. It appeared not as a building but as a model complete with a site map as its base. This was, of course, retroactive and choreographed, but it functioned like a time-lapse film of physical modelling. Displayed this way, the model seemed seamlessly built; all the changes made over the course of time did not have to be registered because it was being 'built' after the fact.

You could level the criticism that the video relied on a conservative notion of model reception; it displayed a digital model in analogue terms. This raises the question as to why a fly-through of a complete digital model is taken as more appropriate to the new technology. After all, the device of the fly-through itself owes its origins to cinema. In the end, the student used the video to resolve his frustrations concerning physical modelling, not digital. Rather than rely on conventional media choices (drawn images and real models), the student used his medium of choice to represent the project in multiple conventions, some tied to drawing traditions, some to analogue modelling, others completely virtual. He made the digital model play against type in the video. In large measure, this made the project exemplary.

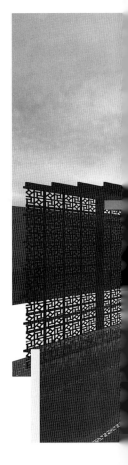

Opposite
The entry to the mosque
cautiously breaks the facade
of the old department store.
The geometry of the doors
hints at the architecture
beyond

Below
A section-perspective reveals
the thinness of the building
envelope and the complex
cascade of floors

Steve Turk

Parenthesis House, Columbus, Ohio, USA   1998

Submitted to the Shinkenchiku Residential Design Competition, Steve Turk's Parenthesis House was designed as a prototype unit to be inserted over a duplex lot on an existing street. The project illustrates the several advantages of computer-aided design not only in terms of its formal derivation, but also in its careful representation:

"The Paren(thesis) House explores issues of pattern making and coding in relationship to the tectonics of dwelling. The house is conceived as two brackets folded out of the site with secondary trays nestled within the resulting shell." [1] The pattern making here is multilayered. Fragments of profiles from Marcel Duchamp's Malic Moulds can be seen in plan and section. There is also the pattern making made possible by the modelling software: a limited number of elements are rescaled, mirrored, flipped and repeated with the touch of a button, giving the house a coherence despite its dynamic spatial configuration.

Two model versions of the final design seem to co-exist, these really being only two directions taken with the virtual model's rendering. There is the shiny version that captures the utterly smooth metallic aspirations for the building's skin. The glass of the many windows and the water in the pool glimmer and reflect. The handrails and window frames cast thin accurate shadows. The aim here is not at verisimilitude, not at a real building, but at a kind of analogue model photograph with no site, no vegetation and no figures cluttering the view. Then there is the non-shiny version of the model which aims more to be a drawing. This model is treated as a graphic which might have been drafted by hand and touched with Pantone. Dashed lines, the absence of shadows, the economy of expression make this model into a series of delicate perspectives, some with silhouetted figures. These include some interesting editing with frame and foreground worthy of Marion Mahony Griffin.

The 'drawings' for the project – plans, sections and an exploded axonometric – all come directly from the digital model which can be sliced into any number of pieces for the sake of conventional drawings. The ground plane of the sections is the dominant graphic feature, tinted grey, and treated

Opposite
Slices of the digital model of Steve Turk's Parenthesis House have been carefully worked over to create these section views

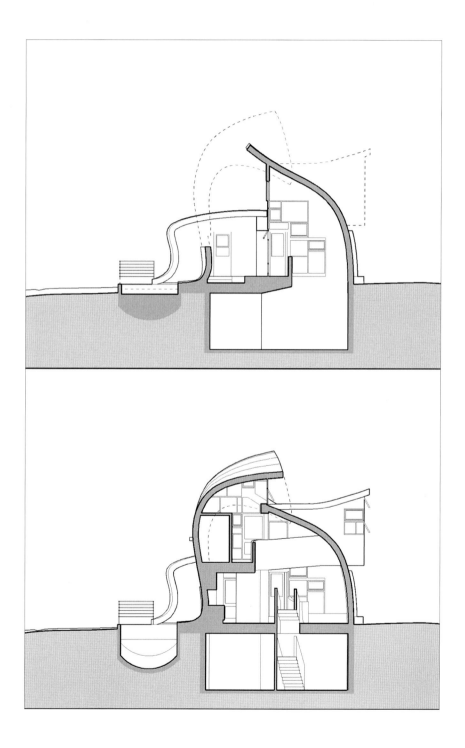

Opposite
Slices of the digital model are
carefully worked over to create
these section views

Below and **opposite**
The plans of both levels
include tints of grey that help
define programmatic zones
and overcome problems with
digital line weights and legibility. Turk's interest in Marcel
Duchamp is clearly evident in
the rendering of level 2 on
the opposite page

Level 1

1 Porch
2 Entry
3 Kitchen
4 Pool
5 Bath
6 Living
7 Storage
8 Deck
9 Lawn
10 Garage

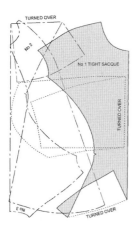

fig.113 After a "Tight Sacque" from Frank
Leslie's Lady's Magazine and Gazette
of Fashion, May 1867

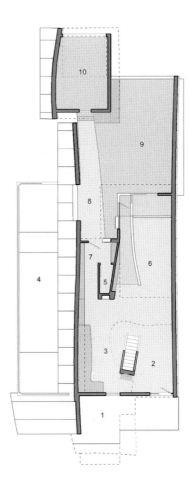

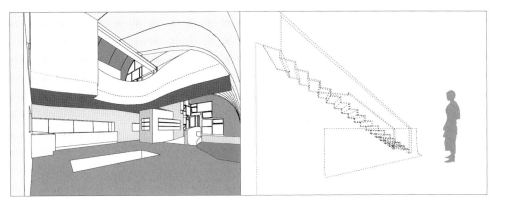

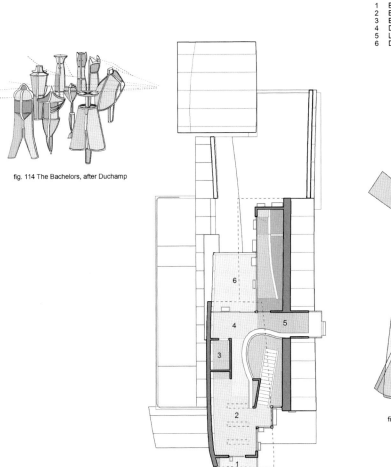

Level 2

1 Balcony
2 Bedroom
3 Bath
4 Dressing
5 Library
6 Deck

fig. 114 The Bachelors, after Duchamp

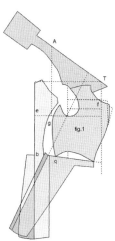

fig. 115 A pattern fragment after
J. Watt, 1822

Below
Another section view. The
architect's graphic sensibilities
come forward particularly in
these views

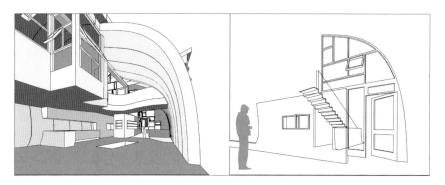

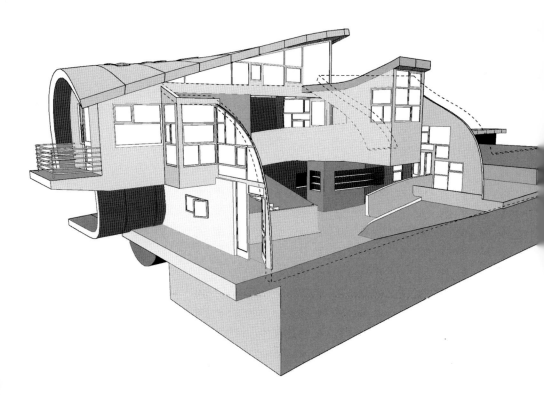

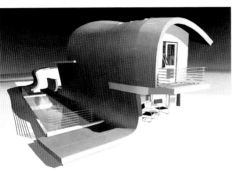

as an autonomous slab (as if we were handling an
analogue section model). An exploded axonometric
hints that it is not actually a drawing or, indeed, an
axonometric projection. It is rendered in perspective
as an exploded model. One expert digital model
is doing all the work, performing every function. In
this, the computer-aided model aids no more, it
fulfils every requirement of a competition board in a
hermetically sealed cycle of modelling, drawing and
visualising; no foreign body, no glue nor graphite,
enters into the equation.

Is this a problem? No. Is this polyglot digital
model easily achieved? No. Turk was trained in
conventional drafting and analogue modelling. His
ability to use this digital model as a convincing
CAD model and a drafting machine is bound to a
(pre-digital) graphic predisposition regarding what
CAD models and standard drawings should look
like and what a competition board should look like.

Part of the strength of the work is down to
representational restraint, showing a complicated
project in a straightforward fashion. Even the
tropes introduced to explain the curves, bends and
geometries of the design are decidedly non-digital,
the 'fabric' of the neighbourhood is answered with
a house that cuts and folds and stitches together
like a garment, a second skin as shelter. The
project is never occluded or led by the digital, but
uses the CAD model as an inexhaustible resource.

Ebru Simsek

Service Pack 4 Robotnik – Gym Updated,
Vienna, Austria   2003

Most computer models are static (which is to say most architecture is represented as static) and any movement associated with these usually comes from the roaming viewpoint of a fly-through sequence. A project that uses movement as a condition of its design, Ebru Simsek's tramcar gym takes advantage of the kinetic potential afforded by digital models and animation software. Sited on a circuit of the street rail system on Vienna's Ringstrasse, Simsek's compact gym fits exercise equipment, showers, lockers and all attendant infrastructure within the envelope of a standard railcar, except that the envelope itself is flexible.

"Training in a gym is a constructed impoverishment of classical spatial experience; it involves a loss of kinaesthetic perception and interaction with the environment. While it is true that certain muscles are specifically trained, they do not react to the world around them: awareness of body, of its demarcation to that which is not the self can only be experienced through bodily movement ..." [1]

Allowing muscle-power to have a direct impact on the environment, the five exercise machines housed in the tramcar are integral to the architecture of the mobile gym. The skin *"transfers and communicates as a membrane the course of every movement; its resistance makes ordinary weights redundant"*. [2] With every movement of the body, there is a reciprocal movement of the exercise machine, which, in turn, pushes or pulls flexible ribs holding the envelope's PVC membrane, altering the interior structurally and spatially.

Simsek's model for the gym includes a series of objects that move; some in tandem, some not. The skin is programmed to react to manipulations of one or more of the exercise machines. Meanwhile, the whole tramcar is also moving on the rails. The animated effect is mesmerising (a convulsing diaphanous green caterpillar), but the project also has to communicate as still images. These might be further annotated to fully illustrate the project. The stills have to be carefully selected as a set, in order for the dynamism of the proposal to be easily read. When single 'shots' are unable to convey the variability of the form, a series of stills has to be organised like a motion picture print. For example,

Opposite
In this perspective, the carriage interior is shown with the exercise equipment specially mounted to flexible structural ribs

Right

A tramcar from Vienne's Ringstrasse is reconfigured as a gym on wheels. The green skin moves with the exercise equipment inside

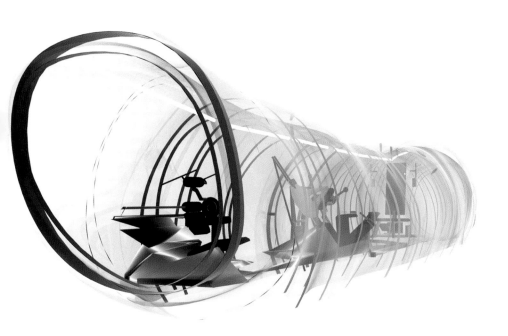

Left
Here the ease of turning off
and on layers of the digital
model helps in communicating
a small but complex project.

Below and **opposite**
More conventional representations of the same virtual
model are overlaid with CAD
drawings

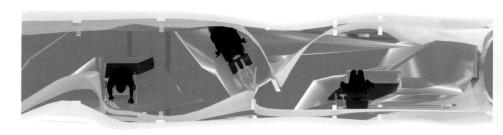

Simsek uses not one but 36 plans of the gym, arranged as a time sequence, to convey the range of motion afforded by the PVC skin.

The challenge here is to show that the project is wildly innovative and, at the same time, insist that the proposal is realisable. To manage this, a typical tramcar is modelled then partially erased leaving the undercarriage. The new design for the gym is grafted on this fragment showing structure, skin and modified exercise equipment. The skin (set at a certain transparency in the model) wraps the ensemble. Ambient and point lighting, shadows and metallic finishes complete the picture. Figures, essential to the idea of the project, are modelled in matte black as pure silhouettes. Interior renderings are further enhanced with the addition of atmospheric effects such as the haze of steam.

The problem with any digital model animation is that it has to compete with or seem commensurate to computer animation in cinema; think of anything from Pixar Animation Studios. This is not a professional requirement, but a precondition of our reception. This creates an unenviable challenge for any architect who wishes to employ computer animation as part of their practice. That said, fellow architects or allied professionals should be able to repress this comparison and see the animation as a representational tool. Clients may have to be trained to see it likewise.

Conclusion
CAM to the Rescue

If CAD adequately replaced scale models, there probably would not be the need for CAM models. But there is a need and CAM does recapture aspects of the standard scale model. CAM can be a real-scale operation, creating prototype parts from a given material. In the hands of architects this same technology can be used to produce miniature or scaled versions of the same. Some CAM processes (the laser and router) are bound to subtractive/routing/carving techniques. Others are additive. Z-starch models are formed topographically. A paste is precisely injected, layer upon layer, into a container of white powder starch. Walls are formed as thin strands of pasted starch one on top of the other. Once the paste has been allowed to set, one simply blows all the loose starch away to reveal a model within, untouched by human hands. This process permits a wide range of forms and is adept at rendering complex interiors. There is the obvious problem of handling them, as the starch reacts to the oil and sweat on one's hands and the model starts to drizzle before your eyes unless treated with a fixative spray. Disadvantages compared with the traditional model are that these are still rather fragile and there is no chance of altering the model.

The CAM model's typical small size is determined by the maximum dimensions of the machine's assembly box. Given this, they are not always built to a scale in the way models traditionally are, their scale is often arbitrary and governed by their manufacture. Students, for example, scale CAM models to get the biggest models they can, given the constraints of the machine. But this is merely a budgetary constraint. Industrial CAM applications are already working at 1:1. *"When artifacts are designed on the computer screen and the design is executed by means of some computer-controlled device, the capabilities of a local craft tradition no longer define the domain of possibilities that a designer can explore."* [1]

CAD-CAM models can be discussed with the help of dichotomies of virtual versus actual and possible versus real. For Gilles Deleuze, the virtual is just as real as the actual, it exists in

memory, in the past and in anticipation. Possibility is actual (it is a possibility right now) but it is not real. Accepting the scholastic maxim that the effect cannot exceed the cause, Deleuze concludes that creative evolution cannot be the movement from the possible to the real, for the possible is not real and cannot cause more reality to come into existence. For Deleuze, the possible is exactly like the real except that it lacks existence. Hence, even if a possibility were to be realised, the process would not be creative: nothing new would emerge. The movement from the possible to the real is then characterised by preformation, resemblance and limitation, for the realisation of one possibility means that other possibilities will not be realised. By contrast, the movement from the virtual to the real is creative, for *"while the real is the image and likeness of the possible that it realizes, the actual ... does not resemble the virtuality that it embodies"*.[2] With no preformed order to dictate the form, the actualisation of virtual being is a creative evolution, an original differentiation of organisation.

The Deleuzean terms can also be used to characterise the different ways in which the architectural model and the computer representation relate to a real building. A computer model is a prime example of the movement from the possible to the real. A good CAD model attempts to present the design as if it were already a photograph of the realised building. Ideally, nothing new is added: the only difference between a good computer simulation and the real thing is that the former lacks existence in the real world. By comparison, the physical scale model allows for much more virtuality, especially the sketch model which functions like a diagram. Moreover, a physical model can be changed intentionally (by the designer, by a critic) or even accidentally (if it falls off the table). CAM mitigates some of the illusionism of CAD by reintroducing scale and, therefore, some level of abstraction even though change necessitates a subsequent model's manufacture.

Architecture and the Miniature

Left and **right**
Student awaiting her laser-cut model pieces. A laser head dances over a sheet of coated plastic set in a vacuum bed. This process emphasises silhouette and assembly

With the analogue model, certain discoveries or decisions about section may arise as the model is built from given plans – with the digital, all orthographic projections must be provided in advance of the mechanical modelling. The grace period a traditional model allows in terms of plastic composition or sculpting of spaces is lost with CAM. The last minute decision or whim is negated; all decisions must pass through the computer rather than the CAM model itself. The CAM model must be allowed to finish before defects or changes can be made and another model built again. In this way CAM makes it difficult to be an architectural *bricoleur*. The laziness of the *bricoleur* demands using what is at hand, what already exists as fragments, but one doesn't assemble CAM models this way. CAD-CAM might promise ease of manufacture, letting the machine model, but this prompts either furtive anticipation (the first time) or tedium (every time thereafter).

Perhaps the most poetic digital device yet to come to the world of the model is the digitiser or microscribe, a mounted stylus used to trace contours of physical objects directly into the computer. Digitisers have been around for decades, the ancestor of every computer mouse, but this new breed is wed to some very nimble software that can interpolate any number of coordinates fed in by the device and easily generate doppelgänger virtual forms that can then be manipulated like any virtual model and output as a fabricated prototype. You can trace your own hand, see the hand on screen as a CAD model and then send it to any CAM machine for a physical replica. More useful, you can pack a digitiser in your luggage, go to some favourite building or monument and trace any part of it in three virtual dimensions. This 'cyber-rubbing' can become a fabricated fragment worthy of Soane's collection.

Part of the appeal of the virtual model and its ascendance over the analogue rests with an architectural quest for morphogenesis or the creation of new forms. Appetite for novelty

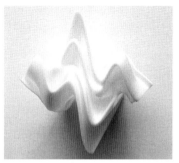

Left

The same form realised with the laser cutter and a rapid prototyping machine. The laser-cut version came out of the machine as a thousand flat pieces that had to be tagged and painstakingly glued; the visual effect being complex and full of refracted light. The version built by a 3-D printer took little student time apart from setting up the model file, but the cost was substantial. The beauty here is that the thin but monolithic, shell-like, shadows are better held by the folds of the object, a more even light suffuses the surface.

Below

A laser-cut site model. Now the norm in both practice and education, laser cutting is characterised by the dense layering of profiles which inadvertently ties model and site together as a condition of their shared manufacture

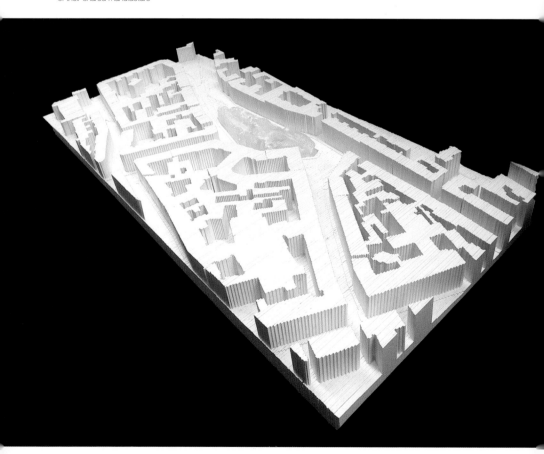

would allow that the physical model has, since the Bauhaus, been thoroughly interrogated. Forms possible with conventional modelling have been exhausted and something new, the computer, is taking over, allowing the introduction of completely new forms. It seems reasonable to suppose that the continued merger of the computer and the model – concatenate CAD-CAM – used 'against the grain' will yield more form variation and, at the same time, reintroduce aspects of the scale model. CAM rescues CAD from dematerialisation and, inadvertently, reinserts scale by virtue of the size limitation of much rapid prototyping equipment. Without CAM, CAD runs the risk of being a high-tech return to Beaux-Arts representation. With CAM, much else is possible, including a new kind of modelling.

Scale models provide tactility and function as a sign of a building in the building's own formal terms, in three dimensions. At the same time the model provides critical distance fostered by the miniature, maintaining a level of abstraction. The miniature offers economies above and beyond those concerned with expense or storage, and economises the reception of a project. It encourages comprehension in front of any real knowledge of the thing itself. The scale model buys critical sympathy. It effects judgment by prompting an intellectual joy or sublime reaction and appreciation for factors such as craftsmanship extraneous to the design idea itself but still a part of architecture as a whole. Around every scale model one could say there is a critical haze generated by miniaturisation. This haze is an integral component of architectural expression, it is the trace of process all the way back beyond the sketch/sketch model to the thought model, the scalar mind of the author.

Keagan Wilson

Drive-through Wedding Chapel,
Las Vegas, Nevada, USA   2003

An architecture student in her second year of college, Keagan Wilson used one project to test several model types and methods of manufacture. Assigned a small wedding chapel off the Vegas strip, Wilson started with the design of a billboard intended to attract customers/impatient couples. She conceived of a kinetic billboard that would lift, unfold and bloom like a desert flower over the course of a day. To model this concept, Wilson built three static versions of the billboard at different stages of 'growth'. This conveyed the idea to peers and professors without requiring her to manipulate a model in front of them. The geometry of the folded plane of the billboard sign suggested an approach to the design of the chapel, giving sign and building formal affinity.

A large site model was built at one-eighth scale by the whole studio ,showing the street, alley-way and adjacent lots (a fast food restaurant and a garage). The space intended for the chapel was left as a hole to be filled by each student. Like many of her studio peers, Wilson initially kept to the formal rhythm of the model streetscape, placing her chapel to the rear of her lot with parking in front. At one point her paper sketch model was moved from the site and later replaced back to front accidentally. Wilson seized on this mistake and reworked her design to incorporate this alternative orientation,

which put the billboard behind the building it was intended to advertise. Undeterred, she resized it so that, from the street, the sign – once bloomed – would appear to just hover over the chapel, visually fusing both, offering a mirage of a bigger building.

The chapel itself was organised into three cubic spaces: lobby and hall divided by a smaller cube meant to showcase the actual ceremony, with a dais for the bride, groom and officiant. The lobby was modelled in basswood where no two walls or ceiling met (corners intended as glass were left as void). The illusion of a floating ceiling plane was managed with internal columns. The ceremonial cube was painstakingly crafted in scaled-down 2x4s, forming three slatted walls.

To create a specific light effect in the hall, Wilson tried to wrap the frame of a cube in thread, twine and even rubber bands, but nothing worked or looked appropriate with the rest of the model. She then turned to the laser cutter, but first had to learn new software in order to program the complex cuts she now wanted to make on planes of bass-wood. The pattern she desired was so delicate that several of the first planes fell apart after being cut by the laser. Wilson had to examine the digital template each time to find the weak link (usually a solid transposed as a void). Once these faults were corrected, the filigree panels could be produced.

Right
Keagan Wilson began her
wedding chapel project with
a blossoming billboard, shown
in model form in three stages
of daily 'growth'

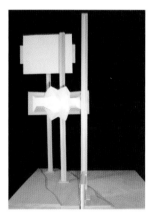

Below
The wedding chapel is set in a
conventional site model showing the adjacent street and the
building's neighbours: a fast
food chain and a garage

Above
Wilson strategically deploys
laser-cut elements where truly
needed (as opposed to wher-
ever convenient). This limited
use of CAM elements in an
otherwise analogue model
makes the lacy chapel visually
and conceptually the most
important component of the
building; a model hierarchy
is achieved

These were materially wed to the rest of the hand-
crafted model, but extraordinary in terms of their
fine detail at that scale.

Had the entire model been laser cut, the hall
itself would have seemed simply more intricately
sliced, but the collage of hand and digital craft, all
in like media, gave the impression that even the hall
was hand crafted. Wilson was quick to explain how
these gossamer walls were made, but the visual
assumption stuck. Much of this perceptual blurring
of analogue and digital was due to the high level
of craft exhibited throughout the whole model. The
analogue bumped the quality of the digital (with a
contrast in perceived density of parts), while the
digital elevated the analogue components (claiming
everything was of the same material order).

The effect of the laser-cut cube in the context
of the rest of the chapel model was doubled when
the chapel was placed in the site model. The project
was never about verisimilitude, but it reached a
level (at eighth-scale) of realism in terms of texture,
light and suggested tectonics. Interestingly, Wilson's
model operates within Alberti's limitations on model
representation: monochromaticity, clear articulation
of parts to whole, interplay of solid and void. This is
a good example of how new modelling technology
might be used strategically. Rather than approach
the laser cutter as a wholesale replacement for
conventional modelling techniques, it was used
where needed as an additional tool.

Opposite
An interior view of the chapel
includes furniture elements.
The wall and ceiling planes
would have been difficult to
achieve without the aid of the
computer and laser

Greg Lynn

Uniserve Corporate Headquarters, Los Angeles, California, USA 1999

Transformation of Kleiburg Housing, Bijlmermeer, Amsterdam, The Netherlands 2001

This project takes computer-aided manufacture to a logical conclusion, blurring the boundaries between modelling and full-scale manufacture. Designing a 4,500 square foot interior to house the Uniserve headquarters within an existing high-rise, Greg Lynn cannot easily manipulate the building's envelope. So, instead, he turns what might be termed his customary process inside out by focusing on the design of an object internal to the envelope that frames, divides and illuminates space. This object houses a conference room and smaller meeting space featured together as a single glowing pod in the middle of the floor: *"The interior layer of the conference room is glass enclosed for sound-proofing purposes and is made up of faceted glass that is set between each structural rib. It floats with the curvaceous and patterned plastic wall as a crystalline gem."* [1]

Lynn's office, Form, is well known for its facility with digital modelling and rapid prototyping. Still, it is surprising to see an office project modelled this way. The model for Uniserve is uncharacteristically conventional, even 'low-tech'. Part of this has to do with an effort to make the architect-designed object special in an otherwise typical environment. To show that contrast, two sorts of models are collided. The floor of the high-rise is simply crafted in card, an extruded floor plan. The conference room form is taken from digital models output to automated routers. The conference room's model walls are

composed of a series of doubly curved plates. These abstract or simplify a much more complex, multilayered, wall section, but they register the general feel and light quality intended. Laser-cut structural rubs are visible through the plastic and the bowed profile of the reception room walls is revealed, as well as the relatively small amount of floor and ceiling space the volume will actually intersect with. Other related elements such as partitions and doors receive similar treatment.

At the scale of the model, the plates that hold the volume of the conference and meeting rooms do not quite align, nor do they enjoy the zero tolerance finesse promised by the thing they mean to represent. Part of this, again, has to do with scale and the degree of abstraction. The real wall sections are meant to be set flush with, not on top of, the structure as they are in the model. Still, the notion that the wall is not truly continuous but segmented is conveyed by the way the model's plastic walls are handled as abutted plates. If the conference room were represented as a seamless monolithic object in the context of the model, it would seem to jump outside the representational language the rest of the model abides by.

Another project, the transformation of the Kleiburg housing block in Amsterdam, is modelled in a similar way but with the focus on translucent panels of stainless-steel mesh applied to the exterior of an existing 500-unit building. Again, with

Right

The model of the Uniserve conference room is realised to a level of detail appropriate to its scale. This prototyped piece, digitally rendered, is not a small version of the actual wall section (which will also be digitally manufactured) but an abstracted version suitable to the requirements of the presentation model

Below

Rapidly prototyped in plastic resin, the Uniserve conference room is framed by a model of the surrounding office floor hand crafted in card

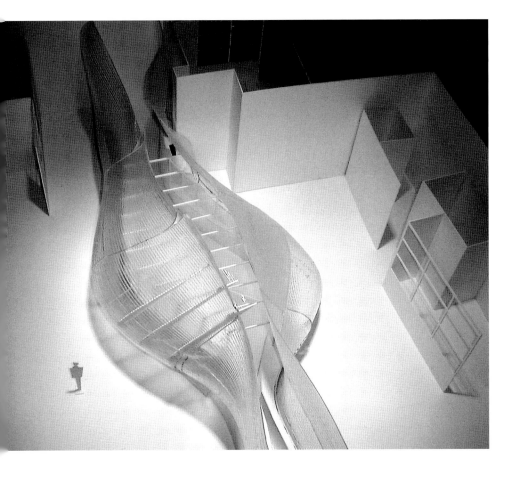

Below

The rear elevation of the housing receives a shallower treatment of prisms that cross floor levels on the elevation

Opposite

This elaborate model of the Kleiburg Housing is made up of a combination of laser-cut, rapidly prototyped and hand-crafted elements. Despite the iridescent sheen of the mesh, Alberti could not fault the model's restraint and overall clarity of intent

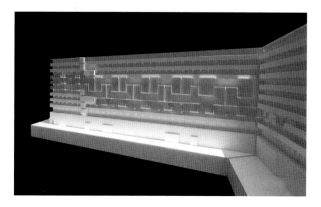

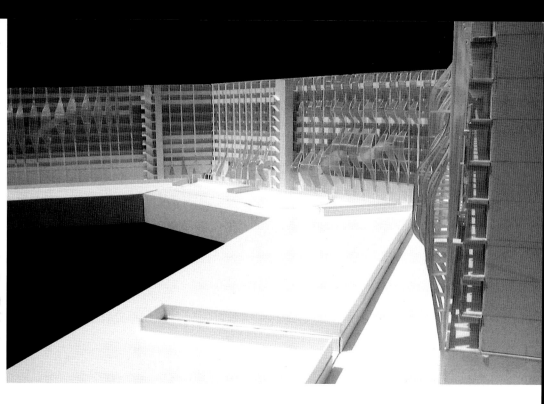

this project Lynn could not greatly alter the building itself. *"The scheme is based on the transformation rather than demolition and rebuilding."* [2] In an effort to overcome the scale of a very large, planned housing estate, he proposed linking small clusters of units with additions of vertical circulation hung off the face of the building. New escalators were to be sheltered from the elements by the panels that in turn would ripple across the whole facade.

Each of the 150 panels would attach to trusses with varying profiles. As with the model for Uniserve, the model for the existing building is restrained and monochromatic. The panels themselves visually pop and shine. The model mesh approximates the mesh intended for use in construction revealing the customised trusses that simultaneously frame and lift. With a relatively light touch, the panels transform the building by dancing across the datum provided by the existing floor slabs and bringing subtle difference to zones of the housing block.

Models for Uniserve and the Kleiburg projects both function to show the contrast between existing and proposed, the everyday and the exceptional. Both models heavily edit the real visual density promised by the designs in favour of clarifying the limited scope of the additions and their more-than-the-sum-of-their-parts impact. These are projects that nestle in or adhere to their built site; both embrace a sense of economy and their models reinforce that sensibility.

Opposite

Panels of metal mesh, each with a unique profile, combine to form vacillating patterns across the exterior of the housing block. The panels also shelter proposed escalators that will cantilever off the facade

Notes

Introduction : To 3D or Not to 3D

1   *Idea as Model*. Institute for Architecture and Urban Studies, catalogue 3, Rizzoli, New York 1980, p 1.
2   Peter Eisenman, letter to various architects, 1976, cited in *Idea as Model*, p 3.
3   'Idea as Model' was in certain respects a reaction to Arthur Drexler's 1975 MoMA exhibition on Beaux-Arts architecture. In his essay for the accompanying book (published in 1977, a year after the 'Idea as Model' show), Drexler writes: *"Architects are seldom interested in metaphysical questions, let alone those raised by three-dimensional models. They may accept enthusiastically the idea that among the 'instruments of thought' language conditions and may even control what may be thought, but the proper instruments of their own thinking – drawing and models – remain largely unexamined. The model is regarded simply as the most convenient surrogate for a reality that cannot otherwise be apprehended whole and without distortion, where the reality is as yet insubstantial."* Architecture of the Ecole des Beaux-Arts, Arthur Drexler (ed), The Museum of Modern Art, New York 1977, p 15.
4   *Idea as Model*, p 1.
5   Diana Agrest, 'Representation as Articulation Between Theory and Practice', in *Practice: Architecture, Technique and Representation – Critical Voices in Art, Theory and Culture*, Stan Allen (ed), Gordon and Breach Publishing Group, Amsterdam 2000, p 164.
6   For example, *The Penguin Dictionary of Architecture*, Penguin, London 1980, compiled by Nikolaus Pevsner, Hugh Honour and John Fleming, has no entry between 'Mnesicles' and 'modillion'.
7   *Idea as Model*, p 17.
8   Mies van der Rohe made a full-scale model of his early Kröller house.
9   Rudolf Arnheim. *The Dynamics of Architectural Form*, University of California Press, Berkeley 1977, p 17.
10 Ibid, p 124.
11 Ibid.
12 Ibid, pp 23-4.
13 Gaston Bachelard, *The Poetics of Space [La poétique de l'espace*, 1958], Maria Jolas (trans), Beacon Press, Boston 1994, p 161.
14 Ibid.
15 Ibid, p 150.
16 Eugene Kupper, 'Nineteen Thoughts on the Model', *Great Models, Digressions on the Architectural Model*, Suzanne Buttolph (ed), The Student Publication of the School of Design, no 27, North Carolina State University, Raleigh 1978, pp 21-2.

17 Tom Porter. *The Architect's Eye, Visualization and Depiction of Space in Architecture*, E&FN Spon, London 1997, p 108.

Chapter 1 : A Model Education

1   Herodotus, writing four centuries earlier than Vitruvius, mentioned ancient model usage when describing the Spartan occupation of Athens (Herodotus, Book V, pp 62–3). See also JJ Coulton's *Ancient Greek Architects at Work*.
2   Leon Battista Alberti. *The Ten Books of Architecture, the 1755 Leoni Edition*, Book II, Chapter I, Dover, New York 1986, p 22.
3   Ibid.
4   Ibid.
5   Ibid, p 23.
6   Comments of the Director to the Design Faculty [attributed to Colin Rowe], 25 May 1954 (copy held in the Hoesli Archives, ETH, Zurich), cited in Alexander Caragonne. *The Texas Rangers, Notes from an Architectural Underground*, MIT Press, Cambridge, MA 1995, p 155.
7   Ibid, p 156.
8   Colin St John Wilson. *The Other Tradition of Modern Architecture, the Uncompleted Project*, Academy Editions, London 1995, p 49.
9   Walter Gropius. *The New Architecture and the Bauhaus*, P Morton Shand (trans), Faber & Faber, London 1935, p 48.
10 Walter Gropius, 'The Theory and Organization of the Bauhaus', *Bauhaus 1919-1928*, Museum of Modern Art, New York 1938.
11 El Lissitzky, *About Two Squares*, 1920.
12 *Dictionary of Architecture*, J Fleming, H Honour and N Pevsner (eds), Penguin, London 1980, p 31.
13 Philip Johnson, letter to David Yerkes, dated 10 January 1933, Philip Johnson Files, Museum of Modern Art Archive.
14 Margret Kentgens-Craig, *The Bauhaus and America, First Contacts 1919-1936*, MIT Press, Cambridge, MA 1999, p 142.
15 Caragonne, p 19.
16 St John Wilson, p 52.
17 It should also be noted that Cranbrook Academy of Art, founded in 1932 outside Detroit, through an Arts and Crafts focus, developed its own distinctive model tradition that persists today.
18 Caragonne, p 17.

UN Studio, Mercedes-Benz Museum, Stuttgart, Germany

1   Ben van Berkel and Caroline Bos. Mercedes-Benz Museum UN Studio office fact sheet.

Chapter 2 : Sketch Models

1   *The Cultures of Collecting*, John Elsner and Roger Cardinal (eds), Reaktion Books, London 1994, p 171.
2   Michel Foucault. *The Order of Things: An Archaeology of the Human Sciences [Les Mots et Les Choses*, 1966], Vintage Books, New York 1973, p 69.
3   'Frank Gehry: Plain Talk with a Master', interviewed by Robert Ivy, *Architectural Record*, vol 5, 1999, p 189.
4   Detlef Mertins and Howard Shubert. *Toys and the Modernist Tradition*, Canadian Centre for Architecture, Montreal 1993, p 7.
5   Norman Brosterman. *Inventing Kindergarten*, Harry N Abrams, New York 1997, p 7.
6   As the first practical proponent of 'natural' education – where the innate desire to learn is nourished and curiosity is unfettered – Pestalozzi abandoned the tradition of interminable lectures followed by student recitation that characterised typical instruction for all age groups, in favour of more active, hands-on activities and what he termed *Anschauung*: 'object lessons' or direct, concrete observation.
7   i.e. an ideal bookless education.
8   Brosterman, p 25.
9   Buckminster Fuller credited Froebel's 'peas work' lesson for inspiring the geodesic dome.
10 Brosterman, p 10.
11 See Frank Lloyd Wright, *An Autobiography*, Duell, Sloan and Pearce, New York 1943, p 34.
12 Ibid, p 34.
13 Caragonne, p 144.
14 Cited in Caragonne, p 145.

Frank O Gehry, Gehry Partners, Walt Disney Concert Hall, Los Angeles, USA

1   'Frank Gehry: Plain Talk with a Master', interviewed by Robert Ivy, *Architectural Record*, vol 5, 1999, p 189.
2   Ibid, p 189.

Le Corbusier and José Oubrerie, Church of Saint-Pierre de Firminy, Firminy-Vert, France

1   A Church for Firminy-Vert [article on-line]; available from *http://cat2.mit.edu/arc/4.204/old_docs/s1996/projects/ phkim/home.html*, Internet, accessed November 2002.
2   José Oubrerie, in interview with the author, tape recording, Columbus, Ohio, 31 May 2002.

Chapter 3. Representational Modes

1   Philip Johnson. Postscript to *Five Architects*, Arthur Drexler, Colin Rowe, Kenneth Frampton and Philip Johnson, Oxford University Press, New York 1975, p 138.
2   Arthur Wortmann. 'Starstruck in Groningen: Hejduk's Wall House Built After All', *Archis*, no 6 , Amsterdam 2001, p 100.
3   Eisenman's House projects have been criticised in much the same way. Another example to consider is Le Corbusier's Esprit Nouveau pavilion. Originally built for the Art Deco exhibition in Paris in 1925, it was a model of an apartment in the larger apartment block. Later in 1977, the pavilion was reconstructed in Bologna. The model is hard to read, and you do not even know what it represents, the Paris pavilion or the apartment block.
4   Christian Hubert. *Idea as Model*, p 17.
5   Christian Norberg-Schulz. *Intentions in Architecture*, MIT Press, Cambridge, MA 1968, p 203.
6   EH Gombrich. *The Image and the Eye: Further Studies in the Psychology of Pictorial Representation*, Phaidon, London 1994, pp 175–6.
7   Rudolf Arnheim. *The Dynamics of Architectural Form*, University of California Press, Berkeley 1977, pp 122–4.
8   Robert Harbison. *The Built, the Unbuilt and the Unbuildable: In Pursuit of Architectural Meaning*, MIT Press, Cambridge, MA 1991, pp 166–7.
9   Jean Baudrillard. 'The System of Collecting', *The Cultures of Collecting*, p 13.
10 Hubert, p 17.
11 Ibid, p 19.
12 Harbison, *Thirteen Ways*, p 205.
13 Peter Eisenman. 'A Poetics of the Model: Eisenman's Doubt', interview by David Shapiro and Lindsay Stamm (New York, 8 March 1981), *Idea as Model*, p 121
14 Elsner, p 175.
15 Ibid, p 164.
16 Harbison, pp 85–6.
17 Lynne Cooke. *Julian Opie*, The South Bank Centre, London 1994, p 64.
18 'Aerodynamic and Aeroacoustic Research', National Aerospace Laboratory (Nationaal Lucht- en Ruimtevaart-laboratorium), article on-line, available from *www.nlr.nl/ public/facilities/f143-01/*; Internet, accessed July 2002.

Zaha Hadid Architects, Placa de las Artes, Barcelona, Spain

1   Thomas Johnson and Mark Morris, '1pm, Cincinnati with Zaha Hadid', *Re:Views*, UIC Press, Chicago 1998, p 10.

Notes – 2

assemblageSTUDIO, Mesquite Fine Arts Center, Mesquite, Nevada, USA

1　Christian Hubert, *Idea as Model*, p 17.

Daniel Liebeskind, World Trade Center, New York, New York, USA and The Jewish Museum, Berlin, Germany

1　See Libeskind's presentation on-line at *www. lowermanhattan.info/rebuild/new_design_plans.*
2　For an interesting argument about the colossal and architecture, see ch 1, part 4, 'The Colossal', in *Jacques Derrida. The Truth in Painting*, Geoff Bennington and Ian McLeod, Chicago University Press, Chicago 1987.
3　One thinks of the very small, gem-like models of Libeskind's collected works commissioned for an exhibition to accompany his 'Micromegas' drawings at the Sir John Soane Museum in 2001.
4　Giles Worsley. 'A Globe Ripped to Pieces', review of the Imperial War Museum North by Daniel Libeskind, *The Daily Telegraph*, Arts section, 29 June 2002.

Greg Snyder with Bill Bamberger, Mobile Gallery, USA

1　Bill Bamberger and Greg Snyder. *Stories of Home and the Mobile Gallery: Photography, Architecture, Community,* College of Architecture, University of North Carolina at Charlotte, Charlotte 2003, p 26.

Coop Himmelb(l)au, BMW Welt, Munich, Germany

1　This sculptural aspect links the architect's conception of a model to that of a sculptor's use of the same term where a model is a preliminary work, say, in wax, from which finished pieces are copied sometimes to the same scale, but often enlarged. Coop Himmelb(l)au's sketch models in foam could be said to operate under both definitions of the term with the final model returning to that equivocal sensibility.

Chapter 4　Model Culture

1　Elsner, p 171.
2　Susan Stewart. *On Longing: Narratives of the Miniature, the Gigantic, the Souvenir, the Collection* [1984], Duke University Press, Durham 1994, p 69.
3　Stewart, p 56.
4　Elsner, p 175.
5　Harbison, p 86.
6　Stewart, p 61.
7　Jonathan Swift. *Gulliver's Travels*, Penguin, London 1994, pp 40–2.
8　A similar sequence is featured in *Rabelais*.

9　Sandor Ferenczi. *Final Contributions to the Problems and Methods of Psycho-Analysis (Gulliver's Fantasies)*, Michael Balint (ed), Eric Mosbacher (trans), Hogarth Press, London 1955, p 48.
10　Gombrich, p 214.
11　Stewart, p 135.
12　Bachelard, p 172.
13　Baudrillard picks up this point: *"There is no real, there is no imaginary except at a certain distance. What happens when this distance, including that between the real and the imaginary, tends to abolish itself, to be reabsorbed on behalf of the model?"* Jean Baudrillard, *Simulacra and Simulation*, SF Glaser (trans), University of Michigan Press, Ann Arbor 1994, p 121.
14　Lévi-Strauss, p 23.
15　Jacob and Wilhelm Grimm. *Kinder- und Hausmärchen, Gesammelt durch die Brüder Grimm*, Berlin, 1822.
16　*Eating Culture*, Ron Scapp and Brian Seitz (eds), State University of New York Press, Albany 1998, p 161.

Peter Wheelwright and Laurie Simmons, The Kaleidoscope House

1　*"To live in a glass house is a revolutionary virtue par excellence. It is also an intoxication, a moral exhibitionism that we badly need"*, Walter Benjamin. 'Surrealism: The Last Snapshot of the European Intelligentsia', *One Way Street and Other Writings*, E Jephcott & K Shorter (trans), Verso, London 1985, p 228.
2　See on-line toy catalogue; available from *www.bozart.com*, Internet, accessed August 2000.
3　Henry-Russell Hitchcock and Philip Johnson. *The International Style* [1932], WW Norton & Co, New York 1995, pp 46–7.

Ben Langlands and Nikki Bell, Logo Works #1 *et al*

1　Alberti, p 22.
2　Ben Langlands and Nikki Bell. 'Millbank' Retrieved, 26 July 2005, from *www.langlandsandbell.com*, accessed 26 July 2005.

Bekonscot Model Village, Beaconsfield, Buckinghamshire, UK

1　Gaston Bachelard. *Poetics of Space,* Beacon Press, Boston 1994, p 159.

Mike McCrary, Mike's Amazing Cakes, Seattle, Washington, USA

1　Marcel Proust. *In Search of Lost Time, Volume II: Within a Budding Grove*, CK Scott Moncrieff and Terence Kilmartin (trans), Random House, New York 1981, p 126.

Michael Cadwell, Pastoral Quartet

1   See definition for folly, at *http://en.wikipedia.org/wiki/Folly.*
2   Michael Cadwell. *Small Buildings*, Pamphlet Architecture 17, Princeton Architectural Press, New York 1996, p 5.

Chapter 5   Virtual Estimations of CAD

1   Stan Allen. 'Terminal Velocities: The Computer in the Design Studio', *The Virtual Dimension: Architecture, Representation and Crash Culture*, John Beckmann (ed), Princeton Architectural Press, New York 1998, p 245.
2   IBM developed the first CAD computer, 'System 2250', in 1964.
3   Allen, pp 254–5.
4   See, Pierluigi Serraino. *History of FormZ*, Birkhäuser Verlag, Basel-Boston-Berlin 2002, pp 5–38.
5   Paul Virilio. 'Architecture in the Age of Its Virtual Disappearance', interview with Andreas Ruby, *The Virtual Dimension*, p 184.
6   Operations in FormZ include: 'Multimodal Design, Assisted Sketching, Information Modelling, Information Filtering, Urban Contextual Databank Systems, Virtual Reality Walkthroughs, Annotation and Sketching on 3D Models on the Internet, Graphics Interpreters of Design Actions, Systems of Diagram Sorting and Analysis, Automated Building Code Checking, Architectural Lighting Design, Lighting Design Evaluation, Shape Grammar, Form-making Algorithms, Form Programming, Regional Environmental Simulation, 2-D Boolean Set Operations, Non-linear Structural Analyses, Airflow Analyses, Route Analyses in Complex Buildings, Interactive Rendering Systems for Animated Assessment, Interactive 3-D Reconstructions for Urban Areas, Evolutionary Automata for Suburban Form Simulation and Polyhedral Objects Controlled by Heteromorphic Effectors'.
7   Allen, p 246.
8   See Robin Evans. 'Translations from Drawing to Building', *AA Files 12*, 1986.
9   Allen, p 246.
10 Ibid.
11 Margaret Wertheim. 'The Medieval Return of Cyberspace', *The Virtual Dimension*, p 55.
12 Lévi-Strauss, p 24.
13 Ibid.
14 William J Mitchell,. 'Antitectonics: The Poetics of Virtuality', *The Virtual Dimension*, p 207.
15 Before CAM applications became widely available to students, casting resins were used to achieve the FormZ look in three dimensions. These tended to look like bits of gelatin which recall the edible models of the previous chapter. Such projects lose something when they become opaque. Students of architecture know the usefulness of synthetic resins to maintain this illusion in miniature. Casting resin is now banned at most schools for its noxious fumes, but there is also an unspoken aesthetic ban operating here disallowing tactile manifestation of purely digital dreamscapes.
16 Allen, p 246.
17 Walter Benjamin. 'The Work of Art in the Age of Mechanical Reproduction' in *Illuminations,* Schocken Books, New York 1969, p 240.
18 Le Corbusier. *Oeuvre Complète*, 1925, pp 65–8, 19, 35, 225; Le Corbusier 1924, p 143; Le Corbusier 1947, pp 106–11.

Jawad al-Tabtaba'i, A Mosque for Dearborn, Michigan, USA

1   Jawad al-Tabtaba'i. *Unfurling Lines: A Mosque in Dearborn, Michigan*, unpublished thesis, College of Architecture, University of North Carolina at Charlotte, 2005, p 1.

Steve Turk, Parenthesis House

1   Steve Turk. *Parenthesis House: Insert (1+(…2)) cut-fold*, unpublished manuscript, 1998.

Ebru Simsek, Service Pack4Robotnik – Gym Updated, Vienna, Austria

1   Ebru Simsek. Service Pack4Robotnik – Gym Updated, unpublished project description, 2005, p 1.
2   Ibid.

Conclusion   CAM to the Rescue

1   Mitchell, p 210.
    Gilles Deleuze. *Bergsonism*, Hugh Tomlinson and Barbara Habberjam (trans), Zone Books, New York 1990, p 97.

Greg Lynn, Uniserve Corporate Headquarters and Transformation of Kleiburg Housing Block

1   Greg Lynn. PDF fact sheet accessed from the Internet, *www.glform.com*, 18 August 2005.
2   Ibid.

CAD-CAM Resources

Modeling Software

Form-Z auto·des·sys,Inc.
2011 Riverside Drive
Columbus
OH 43221
USA
tel +1 614 488 8838
fax +1 614 488 0848
e-mail sales@formz.com
www.formz.com

Rhino 3D
Robert McNeel & Associates
3670 Woodland Park Ave North
Seattle
WA 98103
USA
tel +1 206 545 7000
fax +1 206 545 7321
www.rhino3d.com

SketchUp@Last Software, Inc.
1433 Pearl Street
Suite 100
Boulder
CO 80302
USA
tel +1 303 245 0086
fax +1 303.245.8562
e-mail info@sketchup.com
www.sketchup.com

SketchUp
Atlast Software GmbH
Zeppelinstrasse 71-73
D-81669 München (Munich)
Germany
tel +49 (0)89 45835-471
fax +49 (0)89 44888-96

SketchUp @Last Software Ltd
No 1 Olympic Way
Wembley
Middlesex HA9 0NP
UK
tel +44 (0)20 8434 0518
fax +44 (0)20 8434 0519
e-mail info@sketchup.co.uk

Cinema 4D
Maxon
2640 Lavery Court, Suite A
Newbury Park
CA 91320
USA
tel +1 877-ANIMATE
e-mail Info_us@maxon.net

Cinema 4D
Maxon
The Old School
Greenfield
Beds MK45 5DE
UK
tel +44 (0)1525 718 181
e-mail Info_uk@maxon.net

Maya
Alias
210 King Street East
Toronto
Ontario M5A 1J7
Canada
toll free +1 800 447 2542
tel +1 416 362 9181
fax +1 416 369 6140
     +1 866 226 8859
e-mail awinfo_americas@alias.com

Maya Alias Ltd
1 Newmans Row
Lincolns Inn
Lincoln Road
High Wycombe
Bucks HP 12 3RE
United Kingdom
tel +44 (0)1494 441 273
fax +44 (0)1494 444 867
e-mail infouk@alias.com

Maya Alias GmbH
Betastrasse 13a
85774 Unterfoehring
Germany
tel +49 (0)89 31702-0
fax +49 (0)89 31702-199
e-mail info_germany@alias.com
www.alias-systems.de

3ds Max Autodesk, Inc.
111 McInnis Parkway
San Rafael
CA 94903
USA
tel +1 415 507 5000
fax +1 415 507 5100
e-mail www.autodesk.com

3ds Max Autodesk SA
Rue du Puits-Godet 6
Case Postale 35
Neuchatel
CH-2002
Switzerland
tel +41 (0)32 723 90 00
e-mail www.autodesk.com

CNC Routers

AXYZ Automation Inc.
5330 South Service Road
Burlington
Ontario L7L 5L1
Canada
tel +1 800 361 3408
fax +1 905 634 4966
e-mail sales@axyz.com
www.axyz.com

Techno, Inc.
CNC Router Systems
2101 Jericho Turnpike
New Hyde Park
NY 11040
USA
tel +1 516 328 3970
fax +1 516 358 2576
www.techno-isel.com/CNC_Routers

ShopBot Tools, Inc.
3333B Industrial Drive
Durham
NC 27704
USA

tel +1 919 680 4800
      +1 888 680 4466
fax +1 919-680-4900
email info@shopbottools.com
www.shopbottools.com

Digitisers

Immersion Corporation
801 Fox Lane
San Jose
CA 95131
USA

tel +1 408 467 1900
fax +1 408 467 1901
e-mail info@immersion.com
www.immersion.com

Rapid Prototypers / 3D Printers

Stratasys, Inc.
14950 Martin Drive
Eden Prairie
Minnesota 55344-2020
USA

toll free +1 800 937 3010
tel +1 952 937 3000
fax +1 952 937 0070
e-mail info@stratasys.com
www.dimensionprinting.com

Z Corporation
32 Second Avenue
Burlington,
MA 01803
USA

tel +1 781 852 5005
fax +1 781 852 5100
e-mail sales@zcorp.com
www.zcorp.com

Z Corporation UK Ltd.
Roslyn Works
36 Uttoxeter
Longton
Stoke-On-Trent ST3 1PQ
UK

tel +44 (0)8702 416 502
fax +44 (0)8702 416 503
e-mail sales@zcorp.com
www.zcorp.com

3D Systems Corporation
26081 Avenue Hall
Valencia
CA 91355
USA

toll free +1 888 337 9786
tel +1 661 295 5600
e-mail moreinfo@3dsystems.com
www.3dsystems.com

3D Systems GmbH
Guerickeweg 9
64291 Darmstadt
Germany

tel +49 (0)61 51 357 - 0
fax +49 (0)61 51 357 - 333
e-mail info@3dsystems-europe.com
www.3dsystems.com

3D Systems France Sarl
Parc Club Orsay Universite
Rue Jean Rostand 26
Paris
France

tel +33 (0)1 69 35 17 17
fax +33 (0)1 69 35 17 18
e-mail marketing@3dsystems.fr
www.3dsystems.com

3D Systems Italia srl
via Archimede 42
20040 Agrate Brianza
Italy

tel +39 039 689 0400
fax +39 039 688 1156
e-mail marketing.IT@3dsystems.com
www.3dsystems.com

3D Systems Japan K.K.
4-6-8 Tsurumaki
Setagaya-ku
Tokyo 154-0016
Japan

tel +81 (0)3 5451 1690
fax +81 (0)3 54516630
e-mail japaninfo@3dsystems.com
www.3dsystems.com

Water Jet Systems

Flow
23500 64th Avenue South
Kent
WA 98032
USA

tel +1 253 850 3500
fax +1 253 8139733
www.flowcorp.com

Index

Index – 3

Bibliography

Cultural Aspects

Ariès, Philippe. *Centuries of Childhood, A Social History of Family Life*, Robert Baldick (trans), Random House, New York 1962

Beckmann, John (ed). *The Virtual Dimension: Architecture, Representation and Crash Culture*, Princeton Architectural Press, New York 1998

Elsner, John and Roger Cardinal (eds). *The Cultures of Collecting*, Reaktion Books, London 1994

Grimm, Jacob and Wilhelm. *Kinder- und Hausmärchen, Gesammelt durch die Brüder Grimm*, Berlin, 1822

Mertins, Detlef and Howard Shubert. *Toys and the Modernist Tradition*, Canadian Centre for Architecture, Montreal 1993

Neumann, Dietrich (ed). *Film Architecture: From Metropolis to Blade Runner*, Prestel, Munich 1999

Scapp, Ron and Brian Seitz (eds). *Eating Culture*, State University of New York Press, Albany 1998

Stewart, Susan. *On Longing: Narratives of the Miniature, the Gigantic,the Souvenir, the Collection* [1984], Duke University Press, Durham 1993

Swift, Jonathan. *Gulliver's Travels*, Penguin, London 1994

Taussig, Michael. *Mimesis and Alterity: A Particular History of the Senses*, Routledge, New York 1993

Education

Bauhaus, Fifty Years, exhibition catalogue, Royal Academy of Arts, London 1968

Brosterman, Norman. *Inventing Kindergarten*, Harry N Abrams, New York 1997

Bunch, Michael A. *Core Curriculum in Architectural Education*, Mellon Research University Press, San Francisco 1993

Caragonne, Alexander. *The Texas Rangers, Notes from the Architectural Underground*, MIT Press, Cambridge, MA 1995

Crinson, Mark and Jules Lubbock. *Architecture – Art or Profession? Three Hundred Years of Architectural Education in Britain*, Manchester: University Press, Manchester 1994

Drexler, Arthur (ed). *The Architecture of the Ecole des Beaux-Arts*, Secker & Warburg, London 1977

Fiedler, Jeannine and Peter Feierabend (eds). *Bauhaus*, Könemann, Cologne1999

Gropius, Walter. *Bauhaus 1919–1928*, Museum of Modern Art, New York 1938

Gropius, Walter. *The New Architecture and the Bauhaus*, P Morton Shand (trans), Faber & Faber, London 1935

Kentgens-Craig, Margret. *The Bauhaus and America: First Contacts 1919–1936*, MIT Press, Cambridge, MA 1999

Noffsinger, James Philip. *The Influence of the Ecole des Beaux-Arts on the United States of America*, A Dissertation, The Catholic University of America Press, Washington, DC 1955

Pearse, GE. *Architectural Education, A Survey of the Problem in South Africa, the United States of America, Canada & Europe*, Carnegie Corp., Pretoria 1934

Pollack, Martha (ed). *The Education of the Architect: Historiography, Urbanism, and the Growth of Architectural Knowledge* (Essays presented to Stanford Anderson), MIT Press, London and Cambridge, MA 1997

Teymur, Necdet. *Architectural Education, Issues in Educational Practice and Policy*, Question Press, London 1992

Travers, Wilfrid I. *Architectural Education, A History of the Past and Some Criticisms of the Present System Upon Which are Founded Some Suggestions for the Future with Particular Reference to the Position of the Universities*, Harrison, Jehring & Co, London 1908

Histories

Egbert, Donald Drew. *The Beaux-Arts Tradition in French Architecture*, Princeton University Press, Princeton 1980

King, Ross. *Brunelleschi's Dome: The Story of the Great Cathedral in Florence*, Chatto and Windus, London 2000

Kostof, Spiro (ed). *The Architect, Chapters in the History of the Profession*, University of California Press, Berkeley 2000

Kurrent, Friedrich (ed). *Scale Models: Houses of the 20th Century*, Gail Schamberger (trans), Birkhäuser Verlag, Basel-Boston-Berlin 1999

Hitchcock, Henry-Russell and Philip Johnson. *The International Style* [1932], WW Norton & Co, New York 1995

Millon, Henry A (ed). *Italian Renaissance Architecture, From Brunelleschi to Michelangelo*, Thames and Hudson, London 1996

Millon, Henry A (ed). *The Triumph of the Baroque, Architecture in Europe 1600–1750*, Thames and Hudson, London 1999

Richardson, Margaret and Mary-Anne Stevens (eds). *John Soane Architect, Master of Space and Light*, Royal Academy of Arts, London 1999

Serraino, Pierluigi. *History of FormZ*, Birkhäuser Verlag, Basel-Boston-Berlin 2002

Wittkower, Rudolf. *Idea and Image, Studies in the Italian Renaissance*, Thames and Hudson, London 1978

Wright, Frank Lloyd. *An Autobiography*, Duell, Sloan and Pearce, New York 1943

Theories

Agrest, Diana. *Architecture from Without: Theoretical Framings for a Critical Practice* [1991], MIT Press, Cambridge, MA 1993

Alberti, Leon Battista. *The Ten Books of Architecture* [The 1755 Leoni Edition], *De re aedificatoria* [1485], Dover, New York 1986

Allen, Stan, (ed). *Practice: Architecture, Technique and Representation – Critical Voices in Art, Theory and Culture*, Gordon and Breach Publishing Group, Amsterdam 2000

Arnheim, Rudolf. *The Dynamics of Architectural Form*, University of California Press, Berkeley 1977

Arnheim, Rudolf. *Visual Thinking*, University of California Press, Berkeley 1969

Bachelard, Gaston. *The Poetics of Space* [*La poétique de l'espace*, 1958], Maria Jolas (trans), Beacon Press, Boston 1994

Baudrillard, Jean. *Simulacra and Simulation* [*Simulacres et simulation*, 1981], Sheila Faria Glaser (trans), University of Michigan Press, Ann Arbor 1994

Bois, Yve-Alain. *Painting as Model*, MIT Press, Cambridge, MA 1990

Buttolph, Suzanne (ed). *Great Models: Digressions on the Architectural Model*, The Student Publication of the School of Design, no 27, North Carolina State University, Raleigh 1978

Choay, Françoise. *The Rule and the Model: On the Theory of Architecture and Urbanism*. MIT Press, Cambridge, MA 1997

Deleuze, Gilles. *Bergsonism*, Hugh Tomlinson and Barbara Habberjam (trans), Zone Books, New York 1990

Deleuze, Gilles. *Cinema 1: Movement-Image*, Hugh Tomlinson and Barbara Habberjam, (trans), University of Minnesota Press, Minneapolis 1986

Derrida, Jacques. *The Truth in Painting*, Geoff Bennington and Ian McLeod (trans), University of Chicago Press, Chicago 1987

Drexler, Arthur, Colin Rowe, Kenneth Frampton, Philip Johnson (contributors). *Five Architects* [1972], Oxford University Press, New York 1975

Ferenczi, Sandor. *Final Contributions to the Problems and Methods of Psycho-Analysis*, Michael Balint (ed), Eric Mosbacher (trans), Hogarth Press, London 1955

Foucault, Michel. *The Archaeology of Knowledge* [*L'Archéologie du savoir*, 1969], Routledge Press, London 2002

Foucault, Michel. *The Order of Things: An Archaeology of the Human Sciences* [*Les mots et les choses*, 1966], Vintage Books, New York 1973

Gombrich, EH. *Art and Illusion, A Study in the Psychology of Pictorial Representation* [1960], Phaidon, Oxford 1980, 5th edition

Gombrich, EH. *The Image and the Eye: Further Studies in the Psychology of Pictorial Representation* [1982], Phaidon, London 1994

Haldane, JBS. *On Being the Right Size and Other Essays*, John M Smith (ed). Oxford University Press, Oxford 1985

Harbison, Robert. *The Built, the Unbuilt and the Unbuildable: In Pursuit of Architectural Meaning*, MIT Press, Cambridge, MA 1991

Harbison, Robert. *Thirteen Ways: Theoretical Investigations in Architecture*, MIT Press, Cambridge MA 2001

Hegel, Georg Friedrich Wilhelm. *Philosophy of Right*, TM Knox (trans), Clarendon Press Oxford 1952

Idea as Model. Institute for Architecture and Urban Studies, Catalogue 3, Rizzoli, New York 1980

Bibliography – 2

Le Corbusier. *Towards a New Architecture* [*Vers une Architecture*, 1923], J Rodker, London 1931

Leibniz, Gottfried Wilhelm. *Monadology and Other Philosophical Essays* [1714], Paul Schrecker and Anne Martin Schrecker (trans), Prentice Hall, New York 1965

Lévi-Strauss, Claude. *The Savage Mind* [*La pensée sauvage*], Weidenfeld and Nicolson, London 1966

Porter, Tom. *The Architect's Eye, Visualisation and Depiction of Space in Architecture*, E&FN Spon, London 1997

Porter, Tom and John Neale. *Architectural Super-models*, Architectural Press, Oxford 2000

Wilson, Colin St John. *The Other Tradition of Modern Architecture: the Uncompleted Project*, Academy Editions, London 1995

Wittkower, Rudolf. *Architectural Principles in the Age of Humanism*, WW Norton & Co, New York 1971

Acknowledgements

This book follows doctoral research undertaken in 1998–2003 guided by Mark Cousins, Director of General Studies at the Architectural Association, London, and the late Paul Hirst, first Director of the London Consortium. This work was sustained by a research award from The Royal Institute of British Architects Trust. Much of my own model experience came from teaching opportunities made possible by José Oubrerie at the Ohio State University, Iain Borden at the Bartlett, University College London, Mohsen Mostafavi now at Cornell and Ken Lambla at the University of North Carolina at Charlotte. Jeffrey Kipnis and Neil Spiller have been particularly supportive as readers.

I should thank Kari Jormakka at the Technical University in Vienna along with Steve Connor and Bernard Vere at the Consortium for suggestions and editing of original manuscripts contributing to this text. Jacqueline Gargus introduced me to many models and ideas on our travels. Several colleagues have contributed projects or advice, in particular: Kathy Battista, John Tercier, Barbara Penner, Paul Sutliff, Spela Mlakar, Michael Cadwell, Steve Turk, Greg Snyder, Peter Wong, Chris Beorkrem, José Gámez, Michael Swisher and Dave Lee. My student Gina Robinson good-naturedly volunteered to model CAM equipment. Several other students kindly offered their work.

To my research assistant, Elena Benassi Pupillo, I am truly indebted for her care, calmness and follow-through. This project would have been impossible to complete without her. Several architects and offices generously contributed images and data to this book; Zaha Hadid, Greg Lynn, Jurij Sadar and Bostjan Vuga were particularly helpful early on. Thanks also to Helen Castle for her trust and to my parents, Rick and Barbara Morris, and parents-in-law, Joe and Missy Di Giacinto, for their support. Siblings Molly, Samuel and Sarah were allies in my model childhood and have shown every interest since. Let me finally offer heaps of gratitude to Kathryn and Madelyn Morris for their encouragement and patience.

Photocredits

Cover © Christian Richters *(Exhibition design by Asymptote: Hani Rashid and Lise Anne Couture)*

p 2 © Christian Richters; **pp** 9, 10, 12, 22, 44, 67, 70, 92, 124, 129, 162, 187-9, 191 © Mark Morris; **pp** 15, 122-3, 149 *(top)* © Kathryn Morris; **p** 21 © Markus Breitschmid; **pp** 25-7 © SVA Archive; **pp** 29-31 © Brian Bowman; **pp** 33-5 © UN Studio*; **p** 38 © Chris Beorkrem; **pp** 39, 47-9 © Atelier Wylde-Oubrerie; **p** 40 © UN Studio; **pp** 41, 73, 75-7 102-5 © Zaha Hadid Architects; **pp** 42, 45, 62-3 © Dave Lee; **pp** 51-3 © Gehry Partners LLP; **pp** 55-7 © Atelier de l'Entre; **pp** 59-61 © NOX / Lars Spuybroek; **p** 66 © Renata Hekduk and Collection Netherlands Architecture Institute, Rotterdam ; **p** 69 © Sampson Lloyd; **p** 75 *(bottom)* © Eisenman Architects ; **pp** 79-81 © assemblageSTUDIO / Eric Strain; **p** 83 © Studio Daniel Libeskind; **p** 84 © Jock Pottle; **p** 87 © Skidmore, Owings and Merrill; **p** 88 © Sir John Soane Museum; **pp** 91, 160-1, 163, 167-8 © Michael Ward; **p** 95-7 © Peter Wong; **pp** 99-100 © Bill Bamberger and Greg Snyder; **p** 107 © David Chipperfield Architects; **pp** 109, 111, 113-4 © Coop Himmelb(l)au; **p** 110 *(top)* © ISOCHROM; **p** 110 *(middle + bottom)* © Gerald Zugmann / *www.zugmann.com*; **p** 115 © Volker Moehrke; **p** 118, 145-7 © Bekonscot Limited; **p** 119 © The Royal Archives, Her Majesty Queen Elizabeth II: **p** 120 © Öliblock Inc; **pp** 126-7 © Chu+ Gooding Architects; **pp** 131-3 © Laurie Simmons; **pp** 135-7, 165, 197-9 © Greg Lynn FORM; **pp** 139-43 © Langlands and Bell; **p** 149 *(bottom)* © Mike McCrary; **pp** 151-3 © Mike Cadwell; **pp** 155-7 © Gene Rizzardi / Modelwerkes **pp** 171-5 © Jawad al-Tabtaba'i; **pp** 177-81 © Stephen Turk; **pp** 183-5 © Ebru Simsek; **p** 190 © Chris Herman; **pp** 193-5 © Keagon Wilson

*   The full credit for the images on pages 33-5 reads as follows:
    Mercedes-Benz Museum, 2001-2006, UN Studio © Ben van Berkel, Tobias Wallisser and Caroline Bos, with Marco Hemmerling, Hannes Pfau, Wouter de Jonge, Arjan Dingsté, Götz Peter Feldmann, Erwin Horstmanshof, Gregor Kahlau, Björn Rimner, Alexander Jung, Mike Herud, Thomas Klein, Simon Streit and Taehoon Oh